The Power of Presence

BALANCING YOUR CAREER
&
WELLNESS CARE

TENIA DAVIS, PHD & TRACY GRANBERRY, RDN

CONTENTS

DEDICATION

To our families, whose unwavering love and support have been the foundation of every step we've taken. Your belief in our dreams, even when they seemed out of reach, has given us the courage to pursue them with passion and determination.

To our friends, mentors, and supporters, who have cheered us on, offered guidance, and celebrated every milestone along the way—your encouragement has fueled our ambition and inspired us to keep striving for greatness.

This book is for all of you who have been a part of this journey. Thank you for standing by us, believing in us, and reminding us that no dream is too big when surrounded by a community of love and support.

Tenia & Tracy

A special dedication to one of my greatest cheerleaders — my brother, Billy whose physical presence may no longer be with me, yet I feel his unwavering support and guiding spirit every single day.

Tracy

OPENING:
A SHARED PASSION

Welcome, and thank you for joining us on this transformative journey. It is with great pride, purpose, and gratitude that we bring this program to you, rooted in our shared belief that excellence goes far beyond professional achievements. True success encompasses your whole being—mind, body, and soul—and our deepest intention is to provide the tools that will help you thrive in all aspects of your life.

This project is especially meaningful because it reflects not just our commitment to empowering professionals like you to excel, but also the incredible collaboration I've shared with my cousin and co-author, Tracy Granberry. As family, we share a deep bond and a commitment to supporting one another's growth. Working together on this project has been an enriching experience, blending our individual passions and expertise into something that represents both our professional dedication and our shared values as a family.

I've dedicated my career to helping individuals unlock their full potential, navigate challenges, and find fulfillment in their work and lives. It's a calling I hold close to my heart because I've seen the transformational power of equipping people with the right tools, mindset, and encouragement. Alongside me, Tracy Granberry, a registered dietician and personal fitness trainer has brought over

30 years of invaluable expertise in wellness and well-being, an area where her passion shines so brightly. Her dedication to health, balance, and nurturing the whole person has been a guiding force in shaping this program. She understands that when you care for yourself holistically, you set the foundation for sustained success and joy in all areas of life.

Our shared commitment to our professions and family has made this collaboration an incredible journey—one that we hope will inspire and empower you. As cousins, we've leaned on each other's strengths, found joy in the creative process, and deepened our connection through this shared purpose. This project is not just a reflection of our professional passions; it's a testament to the values we hold as a family: dedication, care, and a belief in the power of lifting others up.

Together, we've created this program as a partnership with you in mind. It's our hope that as you progress through these lessons, you'll feel supported, inspired, and equipped to excel—not just as a professional, but as a whole, balanced, and thriving individual.

Thank you for allowing us to be part of your journey. It has been our privilege to create this for you, and we can't wait to see the incredible things you'll achieve.

INTRODUCTION

Embracing the Journey of Self-Discovery and Goal Setting

Imagine you're on a journey, but you don't have a map, a destination, or even a sense of direction. Without understanding yourself, this journey of life can feel aimless and unfulfilling. Self-discovery and goal setting, however, provide us with both the compass and the map to guide us. *Self-discovery* helps us uncover who we are, what we value, and what drives us, while *goal setting* allows us to channel this self-awareness into meaningful, achievable actions. Together, these two processes create a foundation for a life filled with purpose and fulfillment.

Throughout this book, we'll explore five key steps to help you embark on this journey of self-discovery, clarify your deepest desires, and set meaningful goals that align with who you truly are. For each step, we'll delve into real-life stories, practical applications, and various methodologies you can use to integrate these concepts into your life.

Step 1: Reflect on Your Core Values and Beliefs

Core values and beliefs are the guiding principles that define who we are. They are not just abstract concepts; they shape our decisions, our interactions, and ultimately, our happiness.

Reflecting on and defining our core values is the first step to understanding our true selves.

STORY

Sarah's Journey to Rediscover Her Core Values

Sarah's corporate career had been a whirlwind of promotions, accolades, and relentless hard work. To the outside world, she was the embodiment of success: a corner office, a six-figure salary, and the admiration of her peers. Yet, each morning she found herself staring at her reflection, unable to muster the enthusiasm to face another day. The achievements she once celebrated now felt hollow, like ornaments on a tree that had lost its roots. Deep down, Sarah knew something was missing, but she couldn't quite put her finger on it.

One afternoon, during a rare moment of vulnerability, she confided in her friend Rachel about her feelings of emptiness. Rachel, a life coach and longtime advocate for self-discovery, listened intently before suggesting a simple yet profound exercise: a values assessment. "Sometimes," Rachel said, "we get so caught up chasing what we think we want that we forget to ask ourselves what truly matters." Skeptical but curious, Sarah agreed to give it a try.

Sitting at her kitchen table later that evening, Sarah stared at a list of core values Rachel had shared with her. Words like "achievement," "stability," and "wealth" leapt out—values she had been pursuing her entire career. But as she reflected deeply, she felt little connection to them. Instead, her heart stirred when she read words like "creativity," "community," and "personal growth." Memories surfaced of her college days spent painting murals with friends, volunteering at local shelters, and immersing herself in books about personal development. These moments, she realized, were when she felt most alive. Somewhere along the way, she had let those parts of herself fade into the background.

Armed with newfound clarity, Sarah began envisioning a life where her work aligned with her true values. The idea of starting a nonprofit to support young artists kept resurfacing, tugging at her like a persistent whisper. It was terrifying—she had no experience running a nonprofit and worried about the financial risks. Yet, the thought of empowering others to embrace their creativity felt electrifying.

With cautious optimism, Sarah took the leap. She left her corporate role and poured her energy into building an organization that provided mentorship and resources for aspiring artists. It wasn't easy—there were sleepless nights, funding challenges, and moments of doubt—but for the first time in years, Sarah felt fulfilled. Her work was no longer just a job; it was a calling.

As the nonprofit grew, so did Sarah. She became a vibrant part of her community, surrounded by people who shared her passion for creativity and growth. Each day felt purposeful, a testament to the power of living in alignment with one's core values. Looking back, Sarah realized that her corporate journey wasn't a waste—it had taught her resilience, discipline, and the importance of finding her "why." Now, she was living proof that success is not about climbing the ladder but about building a life rooted in authenticity and meaning.

Through her journey, Sarah learned that rediscovering one's values isn't just about finding purpose—it's about reclaiming joy, connection, and a sense of self. And in doing so, she inspired countless others to pause, reflect, and ask themselves the most important question: *What truly matters to me?*

Application Steps for Discovering Core Values:

1. **Identify Your Core Values:**
   o Start by listing out values that resonate with you. Consider words like "integrity," "freedom," "growth," "security," "adventure," "family," "creativity," and "contribution."
   o After you list 10-15 values, try narrowing them down to your top five.

2. **Ask "Why" for Each Value:**
   o For each of your top five values, ask yourself why it's essential to you. Reflecting on these reasons will reveal the deeper meaning behind each value.

3. **Notice Conflicts in Your Values:**
   o Sometimes, we hold values that may seem to conflict. For instance, you might value both "freedom" and "security." Reflect on how these values can coexist or which one takes precedence in decision-making. Finding harmony between your values can provide clarity in complex situations.

4. **Align Your Goals with Your Values**:
   - ○ Once you understand your values, examine your current goals. Do they reflect your values? Are they guiding you toward a life that will fulfill you? For example, if "adventure" is a core value, setting goals that involve travel, exploration, or learning new skills may feel more satisfying.

5. **Create a Value-Based Vision Board**:
   - ○ Make a vision board centered around your values. Visual representations can help you stay connected to what matters most to you. Use images, words, and symbols that resonate with each core value.

Step 2: Discover Your Strengths, Talents, and Passions

Our strengths and passions form the core of what we can offer to the world. When we align our lives with our natural talents and interests, we experience increased motivation, fulfillment, and success. But discovering these attributes isn't always straightforward.

STORY

Tom's Journey to Discover His True Talents

Tom's life had always felt like a series of checkboxes dictated by someone else's expectations. Graduate high school, earn a business degree, land a stable corporate job—all steps meant to lead him to a "respectable" life. But every day in the office, staring at spreadsheets and attending endless meetings, Tom felt the quiet ache of dissatisfaction growing louder. The problem wasn't the job itself; it was that it didn't speak to him. He often found himself wondering if this was all life had to offer.

The turning point came on a quiet weekend visit to his parents' home. While helping his father clean the basement, Tom stumbled across an old, dusty woodworking kit tucked away in a corner. The sight of it transported him back to his childhood, when he spent countless hours building birdhouses and carving small trinkets with his grandfather. On a whim, he decided to take the kit home and see if he could still create something.

What started as a casual project to pass the time soon became a source of deep joy. Tom lost himself in the process of measuring, sanding, and assembling a small bookshelf. The feel of the wood beneath his hands, the smell of sawdust, and the satisfaction of seeing something tangible take shape filled him with a sense of purpose he hadn't felt in years. He realized that working with his hands wasn't just a hobby; it was a passion that had been buried under years of following someone else's vision for his life.

Encouraged by the spark he felt, Tom took a bold step: he enrolled in a part-time carpentry course at a local trade school. The decision wasn't easy—he feared the judgment of those who might see his move as abandoning his business degree or a "safe" career. But to his surprise, his friends and family noticed how happy and energized he seemed. Their encouragement bolstered his confidence, and Tom soon began dreaming of turning his passion into something more.

As Tom honed his skills, he started taking on small projects for friends and neighbors. What began as a few custom coffee tables and shelves quickly grew into word-of-mouth referrals. Before long, Tom made the leap to leave his corporate job and dedicate himself fully to his craft. He established a small woodworking business, creating bespoke furniture that blended artistry with functionality.

For the first time in years, Tom felt a profound sense of alignment between his work and his true talents. The joy of crafting each piece, coupled with the gratitude of his clients, fueled his determination. His business flourished, not just because of his skill but because of the passion and authenticity he poured into every creation.

Tom's journey taught him a vital lesson: true success is not defined by societal expectations or external validation. It is found in the courage to pursue what makes you come alive. By reconnecting with his love for craftsmanship, Tom discovered not only a fulfilling career but also a renewed sense of self-worth and happiness. Today, his furniture stands as a testament to the beauty of following your heart—and the life-changing power of embracing your true talents.

Application Steps to Uncover Strengths and Passions:

1. **Reflect on Past Experiences**:
   - Think about times when you felt most alive, engaged, or fulfilled. What were you doing? These experiences often indicate our strengths and passions.

2. **Seek Feedback from Others**:
   - Sometimes, others see strengths in us that we overlook. Ask friends, family, and colleagues to share what they see as your unique strengths or contributions.

3. **Take Strengths Assessments**:
   - Assessments like the Clifton Strengths (formerly StrengthsFinder) or the VIA Character Strengths Survey can provide insights into your natural strengths and how to leverage them.

4. **Experiment and Try New Activities**:
   - If you're unsure of your passions, consider experimenting with new activities or hobbies. Whether it's photography, painting, coding, or hiking, trying different things can help you discover what excites you.

5. **Look for Patterns**:
   - Over time, patterns will emerge in the activities that bring you joy and fulfillment. Write down recurring themes or interests and consider how they can be integrated into your life or work.

Step 3: Set Clear and Meaningful Goals Using Multiple Goal-Setting Frameworks

Setting meaningful goals is crucial, but effective goal setting often requires more than one framework. We'll explore the SMART framework, as well as a few others, to provide multiple tools for establishing clear, achievable goals.

STORY

Rita's Success with SMART and OKR Goal-Setting Frameworks

Rita had always dreamed of running a marathon, but without a structured plan, the goal felt intimidating. Her mentor introduced her to the SMART framework: Specific, Measurable, Achievable, Relevant, and Time-Bound. This gave her a clear path to follow. She also used Objectives and Key Results (OKRs) to measure her progress along the way. With each mile she added to her training, she felt more capable and confident, ultimately completing her first marathon six months later.

Application Steps Using Goal-Setting Frameworks:

1. **Use the SMART Framework:**
   - **Specific**: Define your goal in detail. What do you want to accomplish?
   - **Measurable**: Determine how you will measure progress.
   - **Achievable**: Make sure the goal is realistic.
   - **Relevant**: Check that it aligns with your values and current life stage.
   - **Time-Bound**: Set a deadline.

2. **Integrate Objectives and Key Results (OKRs):**
   - Set an overarching objective (e.g., "Build a successful freelance career").

o   Define 2-3 key results that indicate progress (e.g., "Gain three new clients by end of quarter").

3. **Practice "WOOP"**:
   o   **Wish**: Define a wish or goal.
   o   **Outcome**: Visualize the best outcome of achieving it.
   o   **Obstacle**: Identify potential obstacles that might arise.
   o   **Plan**: Create a plan for overcoming those obstacles.

4. **Set Process Goals alongside Outcome Goals**:
   o   While outcome goals (like "lose 10 pounds") are essential, focus also on process goals (like "exercise for 30 minutes daily"). Process goals help maintain consistency.

5. **Use the 10X Goal Method**:
   o   Imagine your goal 10 times larger. By aiming higher, you challenge yourself to think creatively about strategies and stretch beyond your comfort zone.

Step 4: Employ Visualization, Affirmations, and Mindset Shifts

Visualization and affirmations are powerful tools that can help solidify belief in your goals. When practiced regularly, these techniques encourage a mindset that fosters resilience, confidence, and clarity.

STORY

Ben's Transformation through Visualization and Affirmations

Ben had always dreamed of becoming a public speaker, inspired by the way great orators could move audiences with their words. Yet, every time he thought about stepping onto a stage, anxiety consumed him. His palms would sweat, his heart would race, and the mere idea of speaking to an audience felt paralyzing. Ben's fear wasn't just about speaking—it was about being seen, being judged, and potentially failing. Despite his desire to share his ideas, this fear kept him stuck on the sidelines, yearning for change but unsure how to begin.

One day, after yet another failed attempt to volunteer for a speaking opportunity at work, Ben confided in his coach, Mary. She listened to his struggles and offered a solution that felt deceptively simple: visualization and positive affirmations. "Your mind is your most powerful tool," she explained. "If you can train it to see yourself as confident, your actions will start to follow." Skeptical but desperate for change, Ben decided to give it a try.

Each morning, Ben carved out 10 minutes to sit quietly in his living room. He would close his eyes and imagine himself standing on a brightly lit stage, his voice steady and his presence commanding. He pictured the audience smiling and nodding in agreement, fully engaged in his words. At first, the images felt forced, like he was trying to convince himself of something untrue. But Mary had warned him that transformation would take time. Alongside visualization, Ben began repeating daily affirmations, such as "I am a capable and impactful speaker" and "My words inspire and empower others." He even wrote these affirmations on sticky notes and placed them on his bathroom mirror, his desk, and even in his car as constant reminders of his potential.

Over weeks, something began to shift. The visualizations felt more natural, and the affirmations started to replace his inner dialogue of doubt with one of possibility. One day, a small but significant opportunity arose—a team meeting where his boss asked for volunteers to present a new project idea. To his own surprise, Ben raised his hand. Nervous but determined, he used the breathing techniques he had learned during his visualization sessions and reminded himself of his affirmations. Though his voice shook at first, he found his rhythm, and the applause from his colleagues at the end was more than he had dared to hope for.

Encouraged by this small victory, Ben continued to practice and gradually pushed himself to take on larger challenges. Within a few months, he delivered his first formal speech at a community event. As he stood on the stage, looking out at the audience, he realized something profound: the fear that had once controlled him had transformed into excitement. His voice was steady, his heart was full, and for the first time, he truly believed in his ability to inspire others.

Ben's journey was a testament to the power of mindset. Visualization and affirmations didn't just help him overcome his fear; they helped him step into the version of himself he had always aspired to be. His story became a source of inspiration for others facing similar struggles, proving that with patience, practice, and belief in one's potential, even the most daunting dreams can become reality.

Application Steps for Visualization, Affirmations, and Mindset Shifts:

1. **Create a Daily Visualization Practice:**
   - Spend a few minutes each morning visualizing yourself achieving your goals. Imagine the specific details, such as the environment, your emotions, and any sensory elements like sounds or scents.

2. **Write and Use Personalized Affirmations:**
   - Affirmations work best when they are specific to your goals. Create positive statements that reflect your desired outcomes and repeat them daily.

3. **Use a Vision Board:**
   - Gather images, words, and symbols that represent your goals and values. Place your vision board somewhere visible to keep you inspired and focused.

4. **Practice Growth Mindset Affirmations:**
   - A growth mindset helps us see challenges as opportunities for growth. Use affirmations like "I am capable of learning and growing" or "Each challenge is an opportunity to improve."

5. **Reflect on Mindset Shifts Regularly**:
   o Set aside time each week to evaluate your mindset. Journaling about recent challenges and how you approached them can help you recognize progress and areas for improvement.

Step 5: Develop a Resilient Mindset and Build a Support System

Achieving long-term goals is seldom a linear journey. It requires a resilient mindset that thrives on persistence and adapts to challenges. Resilience is the ability to bounce back from setbacks and use them as steppingstones for growth. According to the American Psychological Association (APA), resilience is a skill that can be cultivated through intentional practices such as building self-awareness, maintaining a positive outlook, and embracing change. Research shows that resilient individuals are 60% more likely to achieve their long-term goals compared to those who struggle to recover from adversity.

A critical element of developing resilience is the habit of reflection. Reflecting on past experiences allows us to identify patterns in how we respond to challenges and uncover areas for growth. Journaling, for example, is a proven practice that can increase emotional resilience by 53%, as noted in a study by the University of Rochester. Regularly assessing what works and what doesn't help us adapt our strategies and stay aligned with our objectives. This self-awareness fosters a growth mindset, enabling us to view obstacles as valuable learning opportunities rather than insurmountable barriers.

Building resilience also involves adopting habits that strengthen mental and emotional well-being. Practices such as mindfulness, physical activity, and gratitude exercises are scientifically linked to increased resilience. For instance, a study published in *Frontiers in Psychology* found that individuals who engaged in mindfulness meditation reported a 40% reduction in stress levels, enabling them to tackle challenges with greater clarity. Similarly, engaging in regular physical activity has been shown to boost resilience by releasing endorphins and reducing anxiety.

A resilient mindset alone, however, is not sufficient to achieve sustained success; a strong support system is equally vital. Surrounding yourself with supportive individuals provides emotional encouragement, accountability, and diverse perspectives. Data from a Gallup survey highlights that individuals with close friends or mentors in their professional or personal lives are 22% more likely to accomplish their goals. Whether through family, friends, colleagues, or professional networks, having others to lean on can make a significant difference in staying motivated and overcoming roadblocks.

Best practices for building a support system include cultivating relationships that are reciprocal and based on mutual trust. Join groups or communities that align with your interests and values to expand your network. For instance, professional associations, online forums, or local meetups provide opportunities to connect with like-minded individuals. According to a study by Harvard Business Review, professionals who actively participate in supportive networks are 43% more likely to experience career advancement, which underscores the importance of intentional networking.

Another key aspect of creating a support system is seeking mentorship. Mentors provide guidance, share experiences, and offer feedback, which can accelerate personal and professional growth. Research from the National Mentoring Partnership shows that individuals with mentors are 130% more likely to hold leadership positions in their fields. By fostering relationships with mentors or coaches, you gain access to insights and strategies that can help you navigate challenges and stay focused on your goals.

Combining a resilient mindset with a strong support system creates a powerful foundation for success. While resilience empowers you to persevere through hardships, a support system amplifies your efforts and reinforces your commitment. This combination not only enhances your ability to achieve goals but also improves overall well-being. A study by the Mayo Clinic found that people with strong social connections have a 50% higher chance of living longer and report significantly lower levels of stress.

Ultimately, developing resilience and building a support network requires deliberate effort and consistency. By embracing habits that foster mental strength, reflecting on your journey, and nurturing meaningful relationships, you can create a sustainable framework for achieving your aspirations. As the saying goes, "If you want to go fast, go alone. If you want to go far, go together." Resilience and support, together, are the keys to going far.

STORY

Lily's Path to Building Resilience

Lily had always dreamed of starting her own business, envisioning a life where her passion and work were one and the same. But the reality of entrepreneurship was far from the seamless success she had imagined. Her first product launch flopped, her early marketing efforts fell flat, and potential investors turned her away with polite but firm rejections. Each failure felt like a personal indictment, leaving her doubting her abilities and questioning whether she was cut out for the path she had chosen.

At her lowest point, Lily considered giving up entirely. It was during this time that a friend recommended she attend a workshop on resilience. Reluctant but desperate for guidance, Lily decided to go. The speaker, a successful entrepreneur who had faced her own series of setbacks, shared a simple yet profound insight: failures are not final—they are steppingstones toward growth. "Every obstacle," the speaker said, "is an opportunity to learn, adapt, and move forward stronger than before."

Inspired by the workshop, Lily decided to reframe how she viewed her challenges. That evening, she picked up an empty journal and began reflecting on her recent struggles. Instead of focusing on what went wrong, she wrote about what she could learn from each experience. Why had her product launch failed? Was there a way to better understand her customers' needs? What lessons could she take from the investor meetings to refine her pitch? The act of writing brought clarity and a sense of control, transforming what once felt like insurmountable failures into manageable, actionable lessons.

Lily made journaling a nightly habit, using it as a tool to process her emotions and strategize for the future. Over time, this practice shifted her mindset. She no longer saw setbacks as reflections of her worth but as opportunities to grow. With each journal entry, she began to recognize her own resilience—the ability to face challenges head-on and adapt. Slowly but surely, she applied these insights to her business, experimenting with new ideas and approaching problems with curiosity rather than fear.

Her persistence began to pay off. A revised marketing strategy attracted her first loyal customers, and a carefully honed investor pitch secured the funding she needed. There were still missteps along the way, but Lily now approached them with confidence, knowing she had the tools to navigate them. Eventually, her business took off, not just as a financial success but as a testament to her growth and determination.

Lily's journey taught her that resilience isn't about avoiding failure—it's about embracing it, learning from it, and using it as fuel to keep moving forward. Through her experiences, she discovered that the true measure of success isn't how many times you fall but how many times you rise. Today, Lily shares her story with others, inspiring them to see their own setbacks as steppingstones to a brighter future.

Application Steps for Building Resilience and Support:

1. **Reframe Setbacks as Learning Experiences**:
   o After each setback, ask yourself, "What did I learn from this?" Reflect on how you can apply this lesson in the future.

2. **Practice Self-Compassion**:
   o Recognize that setbacks and failures are part of every journey. Treat yourself with the kindness and patience you would offer a friend.

3. **Celebrate Small Wins Regularly**:
   o Acknowledge and celebrate each small step toward your goal. Celebrating progress reinforces resilience and a positive mindset.

4. **Build Consistent Resilience Habits**:
   o Integrate growth-oriented practices like daily intentions, gratitude journaling, and mindfulness into your routine to strengthen your resilience.

5. **Cultivate a Support Network**:
   o Surround yourself with people who inspire and encourage you. Mentors, friends, and like-minded individuals can offer valuable perspective and motivation during challenging times.

6. **Reflect on Resilience Progress**:
   o Schedule regular reflection sessions to assess your resilience journey. Use a journal to document how

you've grown, areas where you've persevered, and what you've learned.

Self-discovery and goal setting are not single steps but ongoing processes that evolve as we grow. Each time you explore your values, uncover new strengths, or set a new goal; you gain deeper insights into your authentic self. Embrace these processes with curiosity and commitment, knowing that every step brings you closer to a life filled with meaning, purpose, and fulfillment.

From Self-Reflection to Understanding How Others See You

Self-reflection serves as the foundation for personal growth, enabling you to assess your thoughts, behaviors, and experiences. It allows you to identify your values, strengths, and areas for improvement, creating a clearer understanding of who you are. While self-reflection provides invaluable insights, its primary limitation is perspective—you can only see yourself from your own viewpoint. To truly grow and thrive, it's essential to gain external feedback and explore aspects of yourself that may be hidden or unknown. This is where Johari's Window becomes a powerful tool.

Johari's Window takes self-reflection a step further by introducing an interactive framework that incorporates both self-perception and the perspectives of others. By examining four quadrants—what is known to you, what others see in you, what you keep hidden, and what is entirely unknown—it offers a more comprehensive understanding of yourself. This framework emphasizes that growth occurs not only through introspection but also through openness to feedback and willingness to explore untapped potential. Expanding the "Open Area" of Johari's Window allows for greater trust, communication, and self-awareness.

The transition from self-reflection to Johari's Window is an evolution from internal to shared awareness. While self-reflection focuses on personal insights, Johari's Window bridges the gap between your private and public selves, fostering a dynamic exchange of perspectives. By engaging with this tool, you not only deepen your understanding of yourself but also enhance your relationships with others. This transition encourages you to step beyond your comfort zone, embrace vulnerability, and unlock a richer, fuller version of yourself.

Understanding Johari's Window

Johari's Window is a psychological framework developed by Joseph Luft and Harrington Ingham that helps individuals understand their self-awareness and relationships with others. It's divided into four quadrants that represent different aspects of self-awareness and interaction: the **Open Area, Blind Spot, Hidden Area,** and **Unknown Area**. Each quadrant reflects what is known or unknown to yourself and others about your personality, behaviors, or characteristics.

The Four Quadrants:

1. **Open Area**: Represents what is known to both you and others. This includes your shared traits, strengths, preferences, and attitudes. For example, you might know you're

outgoing, and others see you as sociable too. Expanding this area through open communication can strengthen relationships.

2. **Blind Spot**: This quadrant includes aspects of yourself that others see, but you may not be aware of, such as habits, attitudes, or skills. For instance, you might not realize you interrupt people during meetings until someone points it out. Reducing your blind spot requires openness to feedback.

3. **Hidden Area**: Reflects what you know about yourself but choose not to share with others, such as personal fears or insecurities. Reducing the size of this quadrant involves vulnerability and selectively sharing aspects of yourself to build trust and deepen relationships.

4. **Unknown Area**: Contains traits, behaviors, or abilities neither you nor others are aware of. These might include untapped potential, hidden talents, or unconscious fears. Exploring this area often requires self-reflection, experimentation, or seeking new experiences.

The Benefits of Using Johari's Window

The Johari Window is a powerful psychological tool that enhances self-awareness and improves interpersonal communication. Created by psychologists Joseph Luft and Harrington Ingham, it provides a framework to understand how individuals and groups share information and build relationships. Its four quadrants—Open Area, Blind Spot, Hidden Area, and Unknown Area—offer insights into how self-disclosure and feedback can lead to greater collaboration and personal growth. Research has shown that organizations that prioritize self-awareness report 30% better team performance, emphasizing the significance of tools like the Johari Window in fostering trust and efficiency.

Increasing your Open Area, the quadrant representing what is known both to yourself and others, is crucial for transparency and collaboration. Teams with higher levels of openness are 25% more likely to meet their objectives, according to a study published in *Group Dynamics: Theory, Research, and Practice*. Sharing relevant information openly reduces misunderstandings and builds trust among team members. For instance, leaders who share their goals and challenges with their teams create an environment where collaboration thrives, leading to higher engagement and productivity.

Addressing your Blind Spot, the quadrant that represents what others know about you but you are unaware of, is equally important for self-awareness and growth. Feedback is the key to shrinking this area and understanding how others perceive you. According to Gallup, employees who receive regular feedback are 3.6 times more likely to be engaged in their work. Constructive feedback not only helps you refine your behaviors but also improves your ability to navigate interpersonal relationships.

For example, learning about a communication habit that others find unclear allows you to make adjustments, thereby enhancing your effectiveness. The Hidden Area, which contains what you know about yourself but have not shared with others, can also be strategically reduced to deepen connections. Sharing your thoughts, feelings, and aspirations can strengthen relationships and build trust. Research from *The Journal of Experimental Social Psychology* shows that self-disclosure increases feelings of intimacy by 39% in personal and professional relationships. By revealing more about yourself in appropriate contexts, you create a foundation of openness that encourages reciprocal sharing, fostering stronger and more authentic connections.

Exploring the Unknown Area, representing aspects unknown to both yourself and others, is where untapped potential lies. This quadrant can be reduced through self-reflection, experimentation, and seeking diverse experiences. According to a study by the National Institute of Mental Health, individuals who engage in self-discovery activities, such as journaling or skill-building workshops, report a 28% increase in self-efficacy and goal achievement. Venturing into this area may uncover hidden talents, new interests, or innovative solutions to challenges, which can lead to personal and professional breakthroughs.

From a team perspective, the Johari Window promotes a culture of mutual understanding and trust. In organizations that implement self-awareness and feedback models, collaboration improves by up to 40%, according to a Deloitte survey. Teams with reduced Blind Spots and Hidden Areas communicate more effectively, leading to fewer conflicts and higher alignment on goals. Moreover, exploring the Unknown Area collectively can foster innovation by encouraging team members to approach problems from new perspectives and leverage previously overlooked skills.

Finally, the Johari Window supports continuous development and adaptability, two qualities critical in today's fast-paced world. Professionals who regularly engage with self-awareness tools like the Johari Window are better equipped to adapt to change and build meaningful relationships. A survey by Korn Ferry revealed that 79% of employees who consider themselves self-aware report higher job satisfaction and career advancement. By regularly revisiting the Johari Window and integrating its principles, individuals and teams can ensure ongoing growth and resilience.

Johari's Window is more than a theoretical concept—it is a practical tool for unlocking potential and fostering meaningful connections. By increasing your Open Area, addressing your Blind Spot, sharing your Hidden Area, and exploring the Unknown Area, you can achieve greater self-awareness, enhance your relationships, and unlock new opportunities. Whether applied personally or within teams, the Johari Window offers a roadmap to improved communication, trust, and growth.

Johari's Window Exercise

Objective:

To expand your **Open Area**, reduce your **Blind Spot**, and build stronger relationships.

Step 1: Self-Reflection (Open and Hidden Areas)
- Write down 10 traits, behaviors, or skills you believe describe you.
- Highlight those you've shared openly with others. These are in your **Open Area**.
- Identify traits you haven't shared with others—these are in your **Hidden Area**.

Step 2: Seeking Feedback (Blind Spot)
- Select 2–3 trusted colleagues, friends, or family members. Ask them:
  - "What do you see as my strengths?"
  - "What's one thing I could improve?"
- Record their responses, particularly anything surprising or new. These insights reflect your **Blind Spot**.

Step 3: Exploring the Unknown Area
- Identify one new activity or challenge outside your comfort zone (e.g., taking on a leadership role, learning a new skill, or attending a networking event).
- Reflect on what you learn about yourself from this experience. Did you discover any hidden talents or behaviors?

Application in Daily Life

To make Johari's Window a consistent practice, regularly reflect on feedback and experiences. Actively share appropriate aspects of yourself to expand your Open Area and invite honest input from others to minimize your Blind Spot. Over time, this cycle of sharing, learning, and exploring will help you build better self-awareness, stronger relationships, and deeper personal growth.

Career Planning

Career planning is one of the most significant undertakings in a person's life. It is the roadmap to achieving professional success and personal fulfillment. Without clear direction, individuals risk wandering aimlessly, potentially missing opportunities and falling short of their aspirations. Career planning empowers you to align your professional pursuits with your skills, values, and long-term goals, fostering a sense of purpose and satisfaction in your work life.

In today's fast-changing job market, the importance of career planning cannot be overstated. Industries evolve rapidly, new technologies emerge, and the global workforce becomes increasingly competitive. Career planning helps you navigate these changes proactively, equipping you with the strategies to adapt, grow, and excel. This guide will explore the importance of career planning, essential tools and tips, and proven methodologies to set and achieve meaningful career goals.

1. Clarifying Goals and Objectives

At its core, career planning helps you define what success means to you. Success is a subjective concept; for some, it might mean climbing the corporate ladder, while for others, it could involve achieving work-life balance, pursuing entrepreneurial ventures, or making a social impact. Career planning enables you to set clear, actionable goals that align with your personal definition of success.

Without planning, professionals often find themselves in roles that don't align with their aspirations, leading to dissatisfaction and burnout. By identifying short-term and long-term objectives, you can focus your energy and resources on opportunities that move you closer to your desired outcomes.

2. Building Confidence and Motivation

When you have a clear plan, it provides a sense of direction and purpose. Career planning builds confidence because it gives you a roadmap to follow, reducing uncertainty and anxiety about the future. It also keeps you motivated by breaking large goals into smaller, achievable milestones, allowing you to celebrate progress along the way.

For example, if your ultimate goal is to become a senior manager, career planning can help you identify the skills, qualifications, and experiences you need to acquire at each stage of your journey. This incremental progress fosters a sense of achievement and keeps you motivated to move forward.

3. Adapting to Change

In today's fast-paced and unpredictable world, adapting to change has become a cornerstone of career success. The global workforce is continuously reshaped by economic shifts, technological advancements, and evolving societal norms. These changes can be daunting, but career planning offers a structured approach to navigating uncertainty. With a well-thought-out plan, professionals can remain agile, overcome challenges, and seize opportunities without losing sight of their goals.

Career adaptability is about preparing for the unexpected while remaining aligned with your overarching aspirations. Planning isn't just about setting long-term objectives; it's also about building the flexibility to pivot when circumstances demand. Below, we explore how to adapt to changes in the economic landscape, technological innovations, and personal circumstances, along with strategies to maintain resilience and relevance.

3.1 The Importance of Adaptability in a Dynamic Economy

Navigating Economic Shifts

Economic conditions can significantly impact industries and job markets. Recessions, inflation, global trade shifts, and political factors often create fluctuations in demand for certain skills and professions. For example, the 2008 financial crisis reshaped industries, while the COVID-19 pandemic accelerated remote work and digital transformation.

Adapting to these changes requires understanding how economic factors influence your industry. Career planning helps you anticipate potential downturns and position yourself for resilience. For instance:

- Upskilling: During economic uncertainty, acquiring high-demand skills can make you more marketable. For example, professionals in traditional retail transitioned to e-commerce roles during the pandemic.
- Diversifying Skills: Expanding your capabilities to adjacent roles within your industry can increase job stability. A marketing professional might learn data analytics to adapt to a data-driven market.

Building Contingency Plans

Economic shifts often require contingency strategies to ensure career stability. Planning for different scenarios prepares you for potential challenges:

- Plan A: Your primary career trajectory, focusing on ideal goals and milestones.
- Plan B: An alternative path in case of setbacks, such as exploring freelance or contract work.
- Plan C: A safety net, such as developing skills for a different industry entirely.

By maintaining flexibility in your career plan, you reduce the risk of being caught off guard during economic upheavals.

3.2 Embracing Technological Advancements

The Role of Technology in Shaping Careers

Technological advancements are among the most significant drivers of change in the modern workplace. From artificial intelligence (AI) and automation to virtual reality and blockchain, innovations continue to redefine industries. While technology creates new opportunities, it also renders certain roles obsolete.

Career planning in a tech-driven world means staying ahead of trends and embracing continuous learning. For example:

- Anticipating Future Trends: Researching industry forecasts and reports can help you identify technologies that will shape your field. For instance, healthcare professionals might explore advancements in telemedicine, while logistics specialists focus on AI-driven supply chain management.

- Embracing Automation: While automation replaces repetitive tasks, it creates demand for roles requiring creativity, critical thinking, and technical expertise. Adaptability involves positioning yourself in areas that leverage human skills technology cannot replicate.

Upskilling for the Digital Era

Continuous learning is essential to thrive in a rapidly evolving technological landscape.

Strategies include:

- Certifications and Courses: Enroll in programs that teach emerging technologies. For example, IT professionals may pursue cloud computing or cybersecurity certifications.
- Adopting New Tools: Familiarize yourself with software and platforms that enhance productivity in your industry. Marketing professionals, for example, should master customer relationship management (CRM) tools and analytics platforms.

Leveraging Technology for Career Growth

Technology is not just a disruptor but also a tool for advancement. Platforms like LinkedIn, Upwork, and Coursera enable professionals to expand their networks, showcase expertise, and acquire new skills. By integrating technology into your career plan, you can amplify your opportunities and remain competitive.

3.3 Adjusting to Personal Circumstances

Balancing Career and Life Changes

Personal circumstances, such as family responsibilities, health challenges, or relocation, often necessitate adjustments to career plans. Career planning helps you integrate these changes without losing momentum:

- Work-Life Integration: For parents, balancing family commitments with professional aspirations might involve pursuing remote or flexible work options.
- Health and Well-Being: Prioritizing mental and physical health may lead to seeking less stressful roles or jobs with better work-life balance.
- Relocation: Moving to a new city or country might require exploring industries or roles unique to the new location.

Reassessing Goals

Life changes often lead to shifts in priorities. For instance, someone who valued rapid career advancement in their twenties might prioritize stability or entrepreneurial ventures in their forties. Regularly revisiting your career plan ensures it remains aligned with your evolving aspirations.

Seeking Support During Transitions

Navigating personal changes often requires external support. Mentors, career coaches, and peer networks can provide guidance and encouragement during pivotal moments. For instance, a mentor might help you identify opportunities to reenter the workforce after a career break.

3.4 Resilience: The Foundation of Adaptability

Building a Growth Mindset

Resilience is the ability to recover and thrive despite setbacks. A growth mindset—the belief that skills and abilities can be developed through effort—empowers professionals to embrace challenges as opportunities to learn. Career planning with resilience in mind involves:

- Viewing setbacks as temporary and surmountable.
- Seeking feedback to identify areas for improvement.
- Celebrating small wins to maintain motivation.

Developing Emotional Agility

Emotional agility, or the ability to manage emotions effectively, is critical for adapting to change. For example:

- During a job loss, maintaining emotional agility helps you stay optimistic and focused on finding new opportunities.

- In a new role, emotional agility enables you to navigate uncertainties with confidence.

Practices such as mindfulness, journaling, and regular self-reflection can strengthen emotional resilience, enhancing your ability to adapt to change.

3.5 Practical Strategies for Adapting to Change

Scenario Planning

Scenario planning involves visualizing different potential futures and preparing for each. For example:

- Best Case: Achieving a promotion or landing your dream role.
- Moderate Case: Maintaining steady progress in your current role while developing new skills.
- Worst Case: Navigating unexpected layoffs by pursuing freelance or temporary roles.

This proactive approach ensures you are prepared for various outcomes, reducing stress and uncertainty.

Continuous Networking

Networking is a vital strategy for adapting to change. Building strong professional relationships keeps you informed about industry developments and opens doors to new opportunities. Strategies include:

- Attending industry conferences and webinars.
- Joining online communities related to your field.
- Staying connected with mentors and peers.

Regular Career Reviews

Periodic reviews of your career plan ensure you remain aligned with your goals while accounting for changes. Set aside time every six months to:

- Reflect on progress and achievements.
- Assess external changes in your industry.
- Adjust your goals and strategies as needed.

3.6 Case Studies: Adapting to Change

Case Study 1: Thriving During Industry Disruption

When Jane, a travel agent, saw her industry disrupted by online booking platforms, she recognized the need to pivot. Through career planning, she transitioned into a new role as a digital marketing specialist for a tourism company, leveraging her knowledge of the travel industry.

Case Study 2: Embracing Technology for Growth

Raj, a manufacturing supervisor, noticed automation replacing traditional processes. Instead of resisting the change, he pursued certifications in robotics and became a specialist in managing automated systems, securing his relevance in the evolving industry.

Case Study 3: Navigating Personal Challenges

After relocating for her partner's job, Maria, a nonprofit manager, faced limited opportunities in her field. Career planning led her to explore remote work options, allowing her to continue contributing to her organization while adapting to her new circumstances.

3.7 Conclusion: Thriving in a Changing World

Adaptability is no longer a luxury—it's a necessity in the modern workforce. Career planning equips you with the tools, mindset, and strategies to navigate change effectively. Whether it's responding to economic shifts, embracing technological innovations, or managing personal transitions, a proactive approach to career planning ensures you remain resilient and future-ready.

By integrating adaptability into your career plan, you not only prepare for challenges but also position yourself to seize opportunities that align with your goals. Embrace change as a catalyst for growth and let career planning be your guide to a thriving, fulfilling professional journey.

4. Enhancing Professional Development

Career planning is closely tied to personal and professional growth. By mapping out your career path, you can identify skill gaps and proactively pursue learning opportunities, such as certifications, training programs, or mentorships. This continuous development ensures that you remain competitive and relevant in your field.

5. Achieving Long-Term Fulfillment

A well-planned career aligns with your passions, strengths, and values, leading to greater satisfaction and fulfillment. Career planning encourages introspection, helping you uncover what truly drives you and how your work can contribute to your overall happiness and sense of purpose.

WEEK 1

CONFIDENCE IN COMMUNICATION

CONFIDENCE IN COMMUNICATION

Why Communication Matters

Imagine standing in a room filled with colleagues, your palms sweating and your mind racing as you prepare to speak. The question you've rehearsed or the presentation you've meticulously crafted now feels daunting. This moment of self-doubt is something many professionals encounter, yet it underscores an essential truth: communication is more than just a skill—it's a cornerstone of success.

In the workplace, the ability to express yourself confidently and clearly can determine the trajectory of your career. Whether you're leading a high-stakes meeting, pitching a bold idea, or navigating a challenging conversation, how you communicate shapes the perception others have of your abilities. It's not just about the words you use, but also about your tone, body language, and the conviction with which you speak. Strong communicators inspire trust, foster collaboration, and demonstrate leadership in ways that extend far beyond the spoken word.

Effective communication doesn't just open doors—it builds bridges. When you speak with confidence, you're not only sharing ideas but also inviting others to engage, collaborate, and contribute. This builds rapport, strengthens relationships, and creates a foundation of mutual respect. Moreover, confident communication empowers you to tackle obstacles like negotiating a raise or addressing team conflicts with clarity and professionalism. In essence, it transforms challenges into opportunities, helping you thrive both personally and professionally.

In a world where connections drive success, the power of confident communication cannot be underestimated. It's the difference between being heard and being remembered, between merely participating and truly leading. By honing this superpower, you're not just amplifying your voice—you're amplifying your impact.

Building Blocks of Confidence

To communicate with confidence, you must first understand yourself. Confidence isn't about being loud or dominating a conversation; it's about being self-assured in your ability to express your ideas clearly and authentically.

Self-Awareness in Communication

- **Recognizing Your Strengths**: What do you already excel at? Perhaps you're a great listener or you articulate technical ideas well. Build from those strengths.
- **Identifying Triggers**: What situations make you nervous speaking to senior leaders or delivering bad news? Awareness helps you tackle them strategically.

Assertiveness vs. Passiveness or Aggressiveness

Communication exists on a spectrum, with assertiveness serving as the ideal balance between two extremes: passiveness and aggressiveness. Passive communication is often characterized by an avoidance of conflict and a reluctance to express one's opinions or needs. This approach, while sometimes perceived as cooperative, can lead to feelings of resentment, unmet needs, and diminished self-worth. On the other hand, aggressive communication disregards the thoughts and feelings of others, often using dominance, intimidation, or hostility to achieve a desired outcome. While it may secure immediate results, aggressiveness frequently damages relationships, erodes trust, and fosters a toxic environment.

Assertiveness emerges as the sweet spot, enabling individuals to communicate their thoughts, feelings, and needs openly and honestly without encroaching on the rights of others. Unlike passiveness, assertiveness empowers individuals to stand up for themselves, fostering self-respect and personal agency. At the same time, it avoids the pitfalls of aggression by promoting mutual respect and collaboration. Assertive communication is rooted in confidence and clarity, ensuring that both parties feel heard and valued. It creates space for healthy dialogue, encourages compromise, and often results in more sustainable and harmonious outcomes.

The ability to be assertive requires emotional intelligence, self-awareness, and a commitment to maintaining both personal boundaries and respect for others. Techniques such as "I" statements—where individuals express their feelings and needs without placing blame—can help cultivate assertiveness. For example, saying, "I feel frustrated when deadlines aren't met because it disrupts the workflow" is far more effective than an aggressive accusation like, "You never meet deadlines." This approach invites constructive conversation, problem-solving, and understanding, which are hallmarks of assertive communication.

Mastering assertiveness not only enhances interpersonal relationships but also builds confidence and self-respect. It allows individuals to advocate for their needs while fostering trust and collaboration in both personal and professional settings. By finding a balance between passiveness and aggressiveness, assertiveness empowers individuals to navigate challenging conversations with integrity and empathy, creating stronger connections and more meaningful interactions.

Case in Point: Think of Priya, a marketing coordinator. During team meetings, she often avoided speaking up, fearing her ideas weren't good enough. After learning to approach conversations assertively, Priya not only started sharing ideas but also received praise for her innovative input.

Mastering Verbal Communication

Words hold power. The way you say something can make the difference between being understood and being misunderstood.

Articulating Your Thoughts Clearly

When sharing ideas:

- Start with the main point, then provide supporting details.

- Avoid filler words like "um" or "you know." Practice pausing instead—it gives you time to think and conveys composure.

Using Tone, Pacing, and Inflection

Your tone conveys emotions. A warm, enthusiastic tone invites collaboration, while a monotone delivery can alienate your audience. Similarly, pacing ensures your audience can follow along—neither too rushed nor too slow. Inflection helps emphasize key points, keeping your listener engaged.

Quick Exercise: Record yourself explaining a topic. Listen to your tone and pacing. Identify areas to improve and re-record.

The Role of Non-Verbal Communication

Experts suggest that non-verbal cues often carry more weight than spoken words. When your gestures, posture, and expressions align with your verbal message, your communication becomes more powerful.

Key Non-Verbal Techniques

- **Body Language**: Stand tall, but not rigid. Open postures (e.g., uncrossed arms) signal approachability.
- **Eye Contact**: Engage, but don't stare. Aim for 70% eye contact during conversations to show attentiveness.

- **Facial Expressions**: Smile when appropriate to convey warmth and nod to show agreement or understanding.

Example: During a high-stakes client presentation, Ethan, a sales rep, realized he crossed his arms instinctively. After receiving coaching, he learned to use open gestures, making him appear more trustworthy and approachable.

Active Listening: The Unsung Hero

The best communicators are also great listeners. Active listening isn't just hearing words—it's understanding the message behind them.

How to Listen Actively

- **Acknowledge**: Use verbal cues like "I see" or "That makes sense."
- **Clarify**: Ask follow-up questions to demonstrate genuine interest.
- **Summarize**: Rephrase what the speaker said to confirm understanding.

When you listen actively, you not only enhance relationships but also gain insights that make your responses more impactful.

Story: Sofia, a project manager, was known for interrupting her team during updates. After training in active listening, she started letting others finish, leading to better collaboration and fewer misunderstandings.

Overcoming Communication Barriers

Fear is the biggest obstacle to confident communication, but it can be managed.

Strategies to Tackle Fear

1. **Practice in Low-Stakes Environments**: Rehearse speeches or discussions with friends or in front of a mirror.
2. **Shift Your Perspective**: Instead of worrying about how others perceive you, focus on delivering value.
3. **Prepare Thoroughly**: Confidence grows when you know your material.

STORY

Tia's Transformation into a Confident Presenter

Tia, a talented data analyst, excelled at diving into complex spreadsheets and uncovering key insights. But when it came time to present her findings to her department during quarterly meetings, anxiety would take hold. The thought of standing before her colleagues, all eyes on her, made her palms sweat and her voice shake. No matter how well she knew her material, her fear of public speaking overshadowed her expertise.

Determined to overcome this obstacle, Tia decided to take action. She started by breaking her fear into small, manageable steps. First, she practiced in front of a mirror, carefully observing her body language and facial expressions. At first, it felt awkward, but she began to notice areas for improvement, like maintaining eye contact and avoiding nervous gestures. Encouraged by this progress, she took the next step: recording herself while presenting. Watching the playback was daunting at first, but it allowed her to pinpoint areas for refinement, such as pacing and tone.

With her confidence growing, Tia invited a few trusted friends to act as her audience. Their constructive feedback gave her both insights and encouragement. As she rehearsed, she grew more comfortable with her material and learned how to anticipate potential questions, making her responses sharper and more confident. Gradually, what once felt like an insurmountable challenge became a skill she could approach with preparation and poise.

By the time the next quarterly meeting rolled around, Tia was ready. She stood in front of her department, presenting her metrics with clarity and composure. Her confidence radiated, and her colleagues took notice. What started as a personal fear had transformed into a professional strength. Over time, Tia became known not only for her analytical expertise but also for her polished and engaging presentation style.

Tia's journey is a testament to the power of perseverance and the value of breaking big challenges into smaller, achievable steps. By facing her fears head-on and committing to consistent practice, she didn't just conquer her anxiety—she elevated her professional brand and became a role model for others in her organization.

Conclusion: Practice Makes Perfect

Confidence in communication isn't built overnight. It's cultivated through self-awareness, practice, and a willingness to step outside your comfort zone. Start small—choose one conversation this week where you apply a new skill, whether it's assertiveness, active listening, or better eye contact.

Remember, every confident communicator was once a beginner. Embrace the journey and watch as your voice becomes a tool for influence, connection, and success.

WEEK 1 CHALLENGE
Confidence in Communication

Visual Guide: 3 C's of Communication

Step	Action
Clarity	Write key points before any conversation or presentation.
Confidence	Maintain eye contact and steady posture.
Connection	Use active listening and open-ended questions.

Checklist:

- Prepare for a key meeting or conversation.
- Record and review yourself practicing communication.
- Identify one verbal and one non-verbal area to improve.

MINDFUL MOTION: THE ART OF LIVING WELL

Sleep and Quality Rest –
Strategies for improving sleep quality and
establishing good sleep routines.

Affirmation

I will rest my body, rejuvenate my soul, and allow myself to recharge.

Motivational Quote

"Sleep is the best meditation, especially in the fast pace of modern living." The Dalai Lama

Improving sleep quality and establishing good sleep routines is essential for overall health and well-being. Poor sleep can affect mood, cognitive function, immune system strength, and even physical health. Below are effective strategies for improving sleep quality and creating a consistent sleep routine:

Establish a Consistent Sleep Schedule

Set a regular bedtime and wake-up time: The recommended amount of sleep for a healthy adult is at least 7 hours. Going to bed and waking up at the same time every day (even on weekends) helps regulate your body's internal clock. Consistency promotes deeper and more restorative sleep.

Create a Relaxing Bedtime Routine

- Wind down before bed: Engage in calming activities an hour before bedtime, such as reading, taking a warm bath, meditating, or practicing gentle yoga. This helps signal to your body that it's time to relax and prepare for sleep.
- Limit screen time: Avoid exposure to blue light from phones, tablets, computers, and TVs at least 30-60 minutes before bed, as it can interfere with the production of melatonin, a hormone that promotes sleep.

Optimize Your Sleep Environment

- Comfortable bedding: Make sure your mattress and pillows are comfortable and provide proper support. A good quality mattress can make a significant difference in how restful your sleep is.
- Room temperature: Keep your bedroom cool (around 60-67°F or 15-20°C) to promote better sleep. A cooler room is generally more conducive to falling and staying asleep.
- Limit noise and light: Consider using blackout curtains, earplugs, or white noise machines to block out distractions. Keeping the room dark and quiet can help you stay asleep longer.

Be Mindful of What You Eat and Drink

- Avoid large meals, caffeine, and alcohol before bed: Eating large meals or consuming caffeine and alcohol in the evening can disrupt sleep. Caffeine is a stimulant that can interfere with falling asleep, and alcohol may cause fragmented sleep later in the night.

- Stay hydrated, but not too much: Drinking enough water is important, but try to avoid drinking large amounts right before bed to prevent waking up for bathroom trips.

Increase Daytime Exposure to Natural Light

- Get sunlight during the day: Natural light exposure during the day helps regulate your circadian rhythm and promotes better sleep at night. Try to spend time outdoors, especially in the morning, to boost your mood and energy levels throughout the day.
- Avoid bright light in the evening: In the hours leading up to bedtime, dim the lights in your home to signal to your body that it's time to wind down.

Be Active During the Day

- Exercise regularly: Regular physical activity can improve sleep quality and help you fall asleep faster. Aim to exercise for at least 30 minutes most days of the week, but try not to exercise too close to bedtime as it may interfere with sleep.
- Avoid naps late in the afternoon: If you feel the need to nap, keep it brief (20-30 minutes) and avoid napping too late in the day, as this can make it harder to fall asleep at night.

Manage Stress and Anxiety

- Practice relaxation techniques: Techniques such as deep breathing, progressive muscle relaxation, mindfulness meditation, and journaling can help alleviate stress and calm the mind before bed.

- Create a "worry time": If racing thoughts or anxiety keep you up, set aside a time during the day (not right before bed) to write down your worries or work through stressful issues. This can help clear your mind before you try to sleep.

- Consult a doctor: If you have persistent sleep problems, such as insomnia or sleep apnea, it's important to consult a healthcare provider. Underlying conditions may need to be addressed to improve your sleep quality.

Limit Technology Use Before Bed

- Set boundaries with devices: Create a technology-free zone at least 30 minutes before bed to help your body transition to sleep mode. The blue light emitted by devices can interfere with melatonin production, making it harder to fall asleep.

By following these strategies, you can create a sleep-friendly environment and develop healthy sleep habits that enhance your rest. Establishing a good routine takes time, so be patient and consistent with your efforts for the best results.

Weekly Journal Notes

Journal writing can be a powerful tool for self-reflection and personal growth. To get the most out of your journaling practice, set aside a specific time each day to write, creating a routine that fits your schedule. Start with a clear intention or prompt to guide your thoughts and write honestly without self-editing or judgment. Focus on your experiences, feelings, and insights, exploring both positive and challenging aspects of your day.

_____

_____

_____

_____

_____

_____

_____

_____

_____

_____

_____

_____

WEEK 2

TIME MANAGEMENT
& PRODUCTIVITY

WEEK 2
TIME MANAGEMENT AND PRODUCTIVITY

Time as a Non-Renewable Resource

Time is often referred to as the great equalizer because it is one of the few resources that is distributed equally to everyone—each person gets 24 hours in a day. Yet, how individuals choose to spend those hours determines the quality of their lives and the extent of their achievements. Time, unlike money or material resources, is non-renewable. Once a moment passes, it cannot be reclaimed. This reality underscores the importance of treating time as a finite and precious asset, requiring deliberate and thoughtful management. Research suggests that people who prioritize time over money report greater happiness and life satisfaction, emphasizing the intrinsic value of how we allocate our hours.

The challenge with time management lies in balancing productivity with personal fulfillment. Studies show that nearly 40% of people feel they do not have enough time to do everything they need to accomplish, leading to stress and burnout. Effective time management is not about cramming more tasks into an already-packed schedule; instead, it involves identifying and focusing on activities that align with one's goals and values. For example, the Pareto Principle, or the 80/20 rule, suggests that

80% of outcomes often come from 20% of efforts. By identifying and prioritizing these high-impact tasks, individuals can maximize their efficiency while still making room for relaxation and personal growth.

Analytics also reveal that individuals who regularly plan their days and set clear priorities are significantly more productive. According to a study published in the *Journal of Personality and Social Psychology*, goal setting and time-blocking increase productivity by up to 20%, as these practices reduce decision fatigue and procrastination. By taking the time to structure their days around what truly matters, people can eliminate distractions, manage their energy levels effectively, and ensure that their finite time is spent on meaningful pursuits. Recognizing time as a non-renewable resource encourages a shift in perspective—from simply being busy to being intentional, which ultimately leads to a more balanced, fulfilling, and purposeful life.

Imagine Sarah, a marketing manager. She often felt overwhelmed by endless meetings, emails, and deadlines. Despite working late nights, she felt like she wasn't accomplishing much. When Sarah learned to manage her time effectively, she not only regained control of her day but also saw her productivity skyrocket. This week, we'll explore strategies like the ones Sarah used to reclaim her time.

Prioritizing Tasks: The Urgent vs. The Important

Most people spend their days reacting—answering emails, fielding phone calls, and attending meetings—without realizing these tasks aren't always aligned with their goals. Effective prioritization requires discernment: what's urgent isn't always important, and vice versa.

The Eisenhower Matrix

The Eisenhower Matrix is a powerful tool for categorizing tasks into four quadrants:

1. **Urgent and Important**: Tasks that demand immediate attention (e.g., resolving a client crisis).
2. **Important but Not Urgent**: Tasks that contribute to long-term goals (e.g., planning a new project).
3. **Urgent but Not Important**: Tasks that need to be done quickly but don't require your expertise (e.g., replying to non-critical emails).
4. **Not Urgent and Not Important**: Distractions (e.g., excessive social media scrolling).

STORY

When Jack, a junior consultant, began using the Eisenhower Matrix, he realized he was spending 60% of his time in quadrant 3, handling low-priority tasks. By delegating some of these and focusing on quadrant 2, Jack became more effective and even had time to pursue a certification course he'd been putting off.

Building Habits for Productivity

Habits are the foundation of sustained productivity. The best time managers aren't necessarily more disciplined—they've simply designed their days around habits that work for them.

Creating Daily Routines

- **Start Strong**: Use your mornings for high-energy tasks like brainstorming or strategy planning.
- **Plan Ahead**: Spend 10 minutes each evening organizing your next day.
- **End Reflectively**: Review what worked and what didn't, and make adjustments for tomorrow.

The Habit Stacking Technique

Coined by James Clear in *Atomic Habits*, habit stacking involves pairing a new habit with an existing one. For example:

- After brewing your morning coffee (existing habit), review your top three priorities for the day (new habit).

Example: Maria, a financial analyst, struggled to make time for deep work amid constant interruptions. She implemented a "focus hour" after her morning meeting each day, ensuring uninterrupted time for critical tasks.

Overcoming Common Time Wasters

Even the most well-planned day can derail if you're not vigilant about avoiding distractions.

Identifying and Addressing Distractions

1. **Digital Distractions**: Limit notifications, use website blockers, and designate "email check" times.
2. **Unnecessary Meetings**: Before accepting, ask, "Does this require my presence, or can it be addressed via email?"
3. **Task-Hopping**: Multitasking may feel productive, but it often reduces efficiency. Focus on one task at a time.

Learning to Say No

Saying no can be hard, especially in professional settings. However, overcommitting leads to burnout and subpar performance.

- **Polite Declines**: "I'd love to help, but I'm currently focused on [priority]. Could we revisit this later?"
- **Boundary Setting**: Block your calendar for focused work and communicate this proactively.

STORY

Jason, a product manager, used to accept every meeting invite out of fear of missing out. When he began declining non-critical meetings and setting dedicated work blocks, he completed his projects ahead of deadlines for the first time in years.

Balancing Work-Life Demands

All work and no play isn't just boring—it's unsustainable. True productivity includes knowing when to rest and recharge.

Creating Boundaries

- **Work Hours**: Define clear start and stop times. Avoid the temptation to check work emails after hours.
- **Tech-Free Time**: Dedicate specific hours to unplug from devices, especially before bed.

The Power of Rest

Research shows that rest fuels creativity and problem-solving. Consider short breaks between tasks (e.g., the Pomodoro Technique) and regular vacations.

Example: Ayesha, an overworked entrepreneur, implemented "unplug Sundays" where she focused on family and hobbies. The result? Improved focus and energy during the workweek.

Storytelling Example: From Chaos to Clarity

Maya, a busy HR manager, once described her workdays as "putting out fires." Every day, her to-do list seemed endless, and despite working late, she never felt caught up. After attending a time management workshop, Maya made three key changes:

1. **Daily Prioritization**: She identified three must-dos each morning.
2. **Batching Tasks**: Instead of switching between emails and reports, she grouped similar tasks together.
3. **Setting Boundaries**: Maya scheduled her evenings for family time, resisting the urge to "catch up" on work.

In just a month, Maya not only met her deadlines but also found time for yoga classes—a personal goal she'd neglected for years. Her colleagues noticed the shift, praising her for newfound calm and focus.

Take Control of Your Time

Time management is a skill, not a talent—it can be learned and refined with practice. Start small. This week, try one or two of the techniques discussed: perhaps the Eisenhower Matrix or creating a morning routine. Track your progress, and don't be afraid to adjust.

By managing your time effectively, you'll not only accomplish more but also enjoy the journey. As the saying goes, "Don't count the hours—make the hours count."

WEEK 2 CHALLENGE
Time Management and Productivity

Visual Guide: Eisenhower Matrix

Draw a 2x2 grid and place your tasks into these quadrants:

Urgent	Not Urgent
Important	Do first (e.g., deadlines).
Not Important	Delegate (e.g., admin tasks).

Checklist:

- List all tasks for the week.
- Use the Eisenhower Matrix to organize them.
- Schedule daily focus hours for quadrant 1 and 2 tasks.

MINDFUL MOTION:
THE ART OF LIVING WELL

Hydration and the Benefits of Water – The role of hydration in maintaining energy, focus, and physical health.

Affirmation
I drink water to keep my mind and body in harmony.

Motivational Quote
"Water is the most neglected nutrient in your diet, but one of the most vital".– Julia Child.

On average, water makes up to 60% of body weight. It is essential to life. You can survive for several weeks without food, but not more than 3-5 days without water. Staying well hydrated aids in digestion, regulates body temperature, helps reduce the risk of infections, improves cognition and mood.

How much water do you need –

- Eight cups, or 64 ounces daily is a good place to start. The U.S. National Academies of Sciences, Engineering, and Medicine determined that an adequate daily fluid intake is:
- About 15.5 cups (3.7 liters) of fluids a day for men
- About 11.5 cups (2.7 liters) of fluids a day for women
- Athletes, and physically active individuals require more

These recommendations cover fluids from water, other beverages and food. About 20% of daily fluid intake usually comes from food and the rest from drinks.

Best practices for staying hydrated –

- Drink a glass of water first thing in the morning
- Drink when you are thirsty
- Eat foods with a high-water content like fruits and vegetables
- Limit or avoid sweetened caloric beverages
- Drink water with meals, before, during, and after exercise
- Download an app on your smart phone to remind you drink water throughout the day.

Signs of dehydration –

- Thirst is your body's way of telling you to increase your fluid intake.
- Urine color is a quick easy way to check if you are hydrated. Urine should be light yellow, if it looks like apple juice, you are probably dehydrated.

Hydration is not just about quenching thirst; it is an essential element of maintaining energy, focus, and overall physical health. Adequate water intake supports everything from cognitive function and physical endurance to immune defense and joint mobility. By prioritizing hydration throughout the day, individuals can ensure their bodies and minds perform at their best, leading to enhanced well-being and long-term health.

WEEK 3

BUILDING RELATIONSHIPS & NETWORKING

BUILDING RELATIONSHIPS AND NETWORKING

The Power of Connection

The power of connection is undeniable in shaping careers, personal growth, and opportunities. Consider the case of Maria, a talented graphic designer who, despite her hard work and skills, struggled to advance in her career. Her breakthrough came not from additional certifications or countless job applications but from a single connection at an industry event. This creative director, impressed by Maria's portfolio, encouraged her to apply for a role that eventually became the turning point in her professional journey. Maria's story illustrates a fundamental truth: sometimes, opportunities are unlocked not through solitary effort, but through meaningful relationships.

Networking is not about shallow exchanges or collecting business cards—it's about fostering genuine, mutually beneficial connections. Research from the Harvard Business Review reveals that up to 85% of jobs are filled through networking rather than traditional applications. Moreover, LinkedIn's 2023 Workplace Survey found that professionals with strong networks are 68% more likely to experience career satisfaction and upward mobility. These statistics emphasize that building relationships is not just a soft skill—it's a critical success factor in today's interconnected world.

Effective networking requires intentionality and authenticity. While extroverts may naturally thrive in social settings, introverts can also excel by leveraging strategies such as preparing thoughtful questions, focusing on one-on-one conversations, and using digital platforms to initiate connections. Analytics show that 70% of professionals believe networking has directly contributed to their career success, and 61% find digital networking as effective as in-person interactions. Tools like LinkedIn provide opportunities for reaching out to mentors, joining professional groups, and engaging with content that resonates with your goals, making networking more accessible than ever.

This week, we'll explore actionable strategies for building and maintaining meaningful relationships, whether you're a social butterfly or someone who finds the idea of networking daunting. By focusing on authenticity, offering value to others, and staying consistent, you can create a network that not only supports your career aspirations but also fosters personal growth and lasting connections. After all, success is often less about what you know and more about who you know—and how you choose to nurture those relationships.

Relationship-Building Strategies

At the heart of networking is the ability to build authentic relationships. This requires trust, empathy, and a genuine interest in others.

The Role of Authenticity

People are drawn to those who are authentic. Trying to impress others by pretending to be someone you're not often backfires. Instead:

- Be open about your goals and challenges.
- Show curiosity about others' experiences.

Developing Rapport

Rapport-building starts with small yet significant actions:

1. **Active Listening**: Truly hear what the other person is saying without formulating your response prematurely.
2. **Finding Common Ground**: Shared interests or experiences can create an instant connection.
3. **Remembering Details**: Recalling someone's name, a hobby they mentioned, or a project they're passionate about shows that you value the interaction.

Example: Jason, a junior architect, bonded with a senior partner during a company retreat when they discovered a shared love for photography. That connection later led to mentorship and invaluable career guidance.

Networking in Different Settings

Networking happens everywhere—at conferences, in online forums, even at casual gatherings. Knowing how to navigate each setting can enhance your confidence and effectiveness.

In-Person Events

- **Start Strong**: Begin with a firm handshake, a smile, and a clear introduction. For example: "Hi, I'm Sarah, a software engineer with a focus on AI. It's great to meet you!"
- **Ask Open-Ended Questions**: Instead of "Do you like working here?" ask, "What's been the most rewarding part of your role here?"
- **Exit Gracefully**: If a conversation winds down, thank the person and express interest in staying connected.

Quick Tip: If you're nervous, bring a conversation starter. For instance, at a tech expo, you might ask, "Which session has been your favorite so far?"

Online Networking

Platforms like LinkedIn have revolutionized networking, but the rules are slightly different.

- **Personalized Connection Requests**: Always include a note when sending a connection request. Mention where you met or why you'd like to connect.
- **Engage Thoughtfully**: Comment on posts, share relevant articles, or congratulate connections on their achievements.
- **Be Consistent**: Networking online is not a one-time activity. Regularly check in, share updates, and engage with your network.

Example: Alex, a jobseeker, wrote an insightful comment on a LinkedIn post by a hiring manager in his target industry. The manager noticed and invited Alex to apply for an opening—an opportunity that led to his dream job.

The Art of the Follow-Up

The art of the follow-up is a critical, yet often overlooked, aspect of networking. While making a good impression during a conversation is important, the follow-up is where connections deepen, and relationships are truly formed. Networking doesn't end when the initial conversation does; it's the consistent effort to stay engaged and relevant that transforms casual interactions into meaningful relationships. A well-executed follow-up signals professionalism, interest, and respect, often setting you apart in a sea of fleeting encounters.

Timing is the cornerstone of an effective follow-up. Studies suggest that following up within 24–48 hours of meeting someone increases the likelihood of being remembered by 80%. This timeframe ensures that your interaction is still fresh in the person's mind, making it easier to build on the rapport established during your conversation. Waiting too long risks losing the connection altogether, while following up promptly demonstrates enthusiasm and initiative.

Personalization adds depth and authenticity to your follow-up. Generic messages can feel impersonal and may fail to resonate, but referencing specific topics or moments from your conversation shows genuine interest. For example, sending a message like, "I thoroughly enjoyed our discussion about sustainability trends in fashion; your insights were incredibly inspiring," not only reinforces the connection but also opens the door for future dialogue. Research from the *Journal of Business and Psychology* shows that personalized follow-ups can increase response rates by as much as 50%.

Adding **value** to the follow-up can significantly enhance the impact of your outreach. By sharing a relevant article, recommending a resource, or offering assistance aligned with the other person's interests or goals, you demonstrate thoughtfulness and a willingness to contribute to the relationship.

This strategy not only builds goodwill but also positions you as a proactive and resourceful individual. For example, Emma, an MBA student, attended a networking mixer and connected with a startup founder. By sending a thoughtful email with a link to an article on funding trends in their industry, she added immediate value to the relationship. This small gesture not only strengthened their connection but also led to a valuable internship opportunity.

The follow-up is where networking transitions from surface-level to substantial. By being timely, personal, and valuable in your approach, you can turn initial conversations into lasting professional relationships. Analytics support the importance of consistent follow-ups: professionals who follow up effectively are 40% more likely to maintain long-term connections and capitalize on networking opportunities. In the digital age, where meaningful relationships can easily fall by the wayside, mastering the art of the follow-up is an essential skill for anyone seeking to build a strong and supportive professional network.

Overcoming Networking Hesitations

Networking can be a daunting task, especially for individuals who are introverted or feel overwhelmed by the idea of approaching strangers. The perception of networking as an uncomfortable chore often stems from a fear of rejection, self-consciousness, or the misconception that it's purely about self-promotion.

The good news is that networking doesn't have to be intimidating—it can be reimagined as a process of building meaningful, authentic relationships that benefit both parties. By shifting your mindset and adopting practical strategies, you can overcome hesitations and approach networking with confidence.

Tips for Introverts

- offer a roadmap for those who might find large events and social settings exhausting. One of the most effective strategies is to **start small** by focusing on one-on-one conversations or smaller, more intimate gatherings. Research indicates that 84% of introverts find individual interactions more fulfilling than group settings, as these allow for deeper, more meaningful exchanges.
- **Preparing talking points** can also ease anxiety by giving you a framework to guide your interactions. For instance, having a few questions like, "What inspired you to pursue your career?" or "What's the most exciting project you're working on?" ensures you'll always have a conversation starter.

- Additionally, **focusing on listening** rather than speaking shifts the dynamic, allowing introverts to excel by showing genuine interest in others—a trait highly valued in professional relationships. Reframing networking from an act of self-promotion to one of **relationship-building** can also make the process more approachable.

Instead of viewing networking as a means to an end, consider it an opportunity to connect, learn, and contribute. This mindset shift can alleviate the pressure to impress and foster more organic interactions. Asking, "How can I contribute to this relationship?" instead of "What can they do for me?" creates a more collaborative and less transactional experience. Studies show that professionals who adopt a relationship-first approach to networking are 65% more likely to develop long-term connections, according to a LinkedIn Workplace Report.

David's story exemplifies the power of reframing networking. As a software developer, he initially dreaded networking events, viewing them as situations where he needed to impress others with his accomplishments. However, once he shifted his focus to asking thoughtful questions and learning about others' work, he found the process less intimidating and even enjoyable. By relieving himself of the pressure to perform, David was able to form authentic connections that not only expanded his network but also enriched his understanding of his field.

Analytics reinforce the value of overcoming networking hesitations. According to a survey by the Stanford Graduate School of Business, 70% of job opportunities come through personal connections, underscoring the importance of building a strong professional network. Moreover, professionals with robust networks are 58% more likely to experience career satisfaction. By embracing networking as an act of curiosity and relationship-building, even the most hesitant individuals can unlock its transformative potential.

STORY

An Introvert's Breakthrough

Lena, a talented but reserved data analyst, had always shied away from networking events. The idea of mingling in a room full of strangers made her feel uneasy, and she often worried about saying the wrong thing or being overlooked. Instead, she focused on excelling in her work, confident that her results would speak for themselves. But when her company sponsored her to attend a prominent tech conference, she saw it as a chance to step out of her comfort zone and grow both personally and professionally.

Determined to make the most of the opportunity, Lena devised a plan. She started small, choosing a workshop session where group discussions were encouraged. The intimate setting made her feel less intimidated, and she mustered the courage to introduce herself to a few attendees. Instead of forcing conversations, Lena focused on listening, asking thoughtful questions about others' roles and experiences. As she shared her own insights and challenges, she discovered common ground with her peers. To her surprise, one of these conversations led to genuine interest in her latest project—a data visualization tool she had developed to streamline reporting processes.

Encouraged by the positive response, Lena accepted an invitation to present her project during an impromptu breakout session at the conference. Though nervous, she prepared thoroughly and delivered her presentation with passion and clarity. Her work resonated with the audience, earning her not only applause but also meaningful connections with industry leaders who admired her expertise.

After returning from the conference, Lena took the extra step of following up with her new contacts on LinkedIn. She personalized her messages, thanking each person for their insights and sharing updates on her work. Over time, these connections became a valuable part of her professional network. A year later, one of those contacts reached out with an unexpected opportunity—recommending Lena for a position at a leading tech firm. It was a role she hadn't even been searching for, but it aligned perfectly with her skills and aspirations.

Lena's journey highlights the transformative power of taking small, intentional steps to build relationships. By stepping outside her comfort zone and embracing opportunities to connect with others, Lena not only overcame her fears but also opened doors to opportunities she hadn't imagined. Her story is a powerful reminder that networking isn't about being the loudest voice in the room—it's about authentic connections that can shape your career in ways you never expected.

Building Bridges

Building relationships and networking are essential skills that extend beyond professional success—they enrich our lives. Start this week by reaching out to someone in your network or introducing yourself to a colleague you don't know well. Remember, every meaningful relationship starts with a simple conversation.

Networking is not about quantity but quality. Be genuine, be curious, and trust the process. As you cultivate connections, you'll find that the opportunities you seek often come from the people you meet along the way.

WEEK 3 CHALLENGE
Building Relationships and Networking

Visual Guide: Networking Pyramid

1. **Reconnect**: Reach out to 1 current colleague.
2. **Expand**: Add 1 new LinkedIn connection.
3. **Engage**: Attend 1 networking event or comment meaningfully on 3 posts.

Checklist:

- Message a former colleague to check in.
- Share an insightful article or resource with your network.
- Follow up with 1 new connection after a meeting or event.

MINDFUL MOTION:
THE ART OF LIVING WELL

Something is Better than Nothing

Affirmation
I will make exercise a priority.

Motivational Quote
"Some people want it to happen, some wish it would happen, others make it happen." Michael Jordon

Scheduling can be a challenge, but with some planning and flexibility, it's attainable.

Prioritize Your Health - The first step is recognizing that your health and fitness are important.

- Make your workout a non-negotiable priority, just like any other important appointment or task. Once you commit to your fitness routine as a priority, it becomes easier to carve out time for it.
- plan your workouts at times that work best for your energy levels, whether that's first thing in the morning, during lunch breaks, or in the evening.
- Schedule workouts for the week ahead and block out specific times for exercise.

Use Time Blocks - If you can't commit to a full hour, break your workouts into smaller, more manageable time blocks. Even 10 minutes of focused exercise 2-3 times daily is better than nothing.

- Morning: A short, intense workout like a HIIT circuit or a 20-minute jog.
- Lunchtime: A 10-minute walk around the block or a quick bodyweight routine (e.g., squats, push-ups, lunges).
- Evening: A stretching routine or yoga for relaxation, or a more extended session if you have the time.

Make It Social

- If socializing is a part of your busy life, try incorporating exercise into your social calendar. Invite friends or family members to join you for a walk, hike, or even a fitness class. It's a great way to stay connected while also being active.

Set Realistic Expectations

- Remember, perfection isn't the goal—consistency is. You don't need to work out for an hour every single day. Even short, consistent workouts are highly effective for long-term fitness. Be kind to yourself if you miss a session or have to shorten your workout.

By planning ahead, staying flexible, and finding ways to make exercise a regular part of your day, you can work around a busy schedule while still making fitness a priority.

WEEK 4

EFFECTIVE
GOAL SETTING &
PRIORITIZATION

EFFECTIVE GOAL SETTING AND PRIORITIZATION

Turning Aspirations into Achievements

Turning aspirations into achievements is a skill that differentiates those who dream from those who succeed. The key lies in effective goal setting and prioritization, which transform vague desires into actionable, measurable steps. Without a structured approach, even the most ambitious dreams can remain just that—dreams. Studies from the *American Psychological Association* show that individuals who set specific goals are 10 times more likely to achieve them than those with undefined aspirations.

This week, we'll dive into the strategies that can turn lofty ambitions into tangible accomplishments.

Take Adam, a software engineer with aspirations of becoming a project manager. For years, Adam repeatedly told himself, "I'll work toward it someday," but that someday never arrived because he lacked a plan. This is a common pitfall; research from *Forbes* reveals that 92% of people fail to achieve their New Year's resolutions, often due to a lack of specificity and follow-through. Adam's turning point came when he started mapping out a clear path toward his goal. He set measurable milestones, such as earning certifications, seeking mentorship, and volunteering for leadership roles. Each step brought him closer to his ultimate objective, proving that well-defined goals paired with actionable steps lead to success.

Setting meaningful goals begins with the SMART framework: goals should be Specific, Measurable, Achievable, Relevant, and Time-bound. For instance, rather than saying, "I want to advance in my career," a SMART goal would be, "I will complete a leadership certification course within six months." This approach provides clarity and a timeline, keeping you focused and accountable. Analytics support the effectiveness of this method: according to a study published in *Harvard Business Review*, individuals who write down their goals are 33% more likely to achieve them, and those who share their progress with an accountability partner increase their success rate by 76%.

Prioritization is equally crucial to goal achievement, especially in today's fast-paced, multitasking environment. The Eisenhower Matrix—a tool that categorizes tasks based on urgency and importance—can help individuals focus on what truly matters and avoid getting bogged down by distractions. For example, tasks that are both urgent and important, like preparing for a meeting, should be tackled immediately, while important but non-urgent tasks, like developing long-term skills, can be scheduled. Analytics from *McKinsey & Company* show that effective prioritization can increase productivity by up to 25%, as it ensures energy and resources are allocated to tasks that align with overarching goals.

This week, we'll explore practical strategies for setting goals, prioritizing effectively, and overcoming challenges like procrastination and burnout. Whether you're striving for career advancement, personal development, or organizational success, mastering goal setting and prioritization can help you turn aspirations into achievements, ensuring that your efforts yield meaningful and lasting results.

The Framework of Goal Setting

Goals are most effective when they are clear, actionable, and aligned with your values. This is where frameworks like SMART goals come into play.

What Are SMART Goals?

SMART goals are:

1. **Specific**: Clearly define what you want to achieve.
   - Instead of "I want to get fit," try "I want to run a 5K race in three months."
2. **Measurable**: Include metrics to track progress.
   - For example, "I will complete three 5K training sessions per week."
3. **Achievable**: Ensure the goal is realistic given your current resources and constraints.
4. **Relevant**: Align the goal with your long-term objectives and values.
5. **Time-Bound**: Set a deadline to create urgency.

Example: Sarah, a marketing associate, wanted to boost her visibility at work. Her SMART goal: "Lead a presentation on digital trends at next quarter's team meeting." This gave her a clear, actionable path to success.

Aligning Goals with Values

A goal that aligns with your core values will feel more meaningful, making it easier to stay committed. Ask yourself:

- "Why is this goal important to me?"
- "How does it contribute to my broader aspirations?"

Breaking Goals into Manageable Steps

Large goals can feel daunting unless broken into smaller, actionable steps.

Creating Action Plans

- **Start with a Mind Map**: Visualize your goal and the steps required to achieve it.
- **Build a Timeline**: Use Gantt charts or calendar tools to set milestones.
- **Assign Microtasks**: Break each milestone into daily or weekly actions.

Example: When Priya decided to launch her small business, she didn't tackle it all at once. She divided her goal into phases: market research, product development, and soft launching. Each phase was further broken into manageable tasks, keeping her on track without overwhelm.

Setting Milestones

Milestones act as checkpoints to measure progress and celebrate achievements. For instance:

- Milestone 1: Complete a business plan.
- Milestone 2: Develop a prototype.
- Milestone 3: Secure initial funding.

The Art of Prioritization

In a world filled with competing demands, prioritization is key to ensuring your goals remain in focus.

Techniques for Prioritizing Tasks

1. **ABCDE Method**:
   - **A**: Must do—critical tasks with high consequences.
   - **B**: Should do—important but less urgent tasks.
   - **C**: Nice to do—low-impact activities.
   - **D**: Delegate—tasks someone else can handle.
   - **E**: Eliminate—unnecessary tasks.

2. **Pareto Principle (80/20 Rule)**:
   - Focus on the 20% of tasks that produce 80% of results. For example, a sales professional might prioritize engaging with key clients rather than attending every meeting.

Balancing Competing Priorities

When everything feels urgent, consider:

- **Deadlines**: What needs immediate attention?
- **Impact**: Which tasks will have the most significant outcomes?
- **Energy Levels**: Schedule high-focus tasks during peak productivity times.

Example: Mark, a project manager, used to juggle too many tasks at once. By applying the ABCDE method, he identified which responsibilities required his direct input and delegated the rest. This allowed him to focus on high-priority deliverables, increasing his efficiency and team satisfaction.

Overcoming Goal-Setting Challenges

Even the best plans can face hurdles. The key is to anticipate and address these obstacles proactively.

Combatting Procrastination

- **Use the Two-Minute Rule**: If a task takes less than two minutes, do it immediately.
- **Focus on the First Step**: Instead of thinking about the entire project, concentrate on starting.

Handling Setbacks

Setbacks are inevitable, but they don't have to derail your progress.

- **Reassess Your Plan**: Adjust timelines or methods as needed.
- **Learn from Challenges**: Reflect on what went wrong and how to improve.

Adapting to Shifting Priorities

Life happens—new responsibilities or unexpected opportunities may require you to pivot.

- **Revisit Your Goals**: Are they still relevant? If not, adjust them.
- **Stay Flexible**: Adapt without abandoning your overall vision.

STORY

From Setbacks to Strategic Success

Emma, a seasoned sales director, and James, a diligent team lead, both faced challenges that tested their resilience and leadership. Though their struggles were different, their stories reveal the transformative power of focus, strategy, and perseverance in overcoming professional hurdles.

Emma encountered a major setback when a high-profile client deal, months in the making, unexpectedly fell through. The loss stung—not just financially but emotionally, as she had poured her energy into securing the agreement. Instead of dwelling on the disappointment, Emma made a deliberate choice to refocus. Drawing on her experience, she identified five promising prospects in her pipeline and committed to strengthening relationships with each of them. By tailoring her pitches, listening closely to client needs, and following up diligently, she not only recovered from the initial loss but exceeded her quarterly sales targets by 25%. Emma's setback became a catalyst for growth, proving that resilience and a proactive mindset can turn challenges into triumphs.

James faced a different challenge: disorganization. As a team lead, he had the technical expertise to excel, but his lack of structure created chaos. He approached each day without a clear plan, addressing tasks as they arose. Over time, this reactive approach led to missed deadlines and frustration within his team. Recognizing the need for change, James attended a workshop on goal setting. He was introduced to SMART goals (Specific, Measurable, Achievable, Relevant, Time-bound) and the ABCDE prioritization method, which assigns tasks based on urgency and importance.

Armed with these tools, James implemented a plan to streamline his team's workflow. He set a SMART goal to reduce turnaround times by 20% within three months. To achieve this, he mapped out key processes, delegated tasks based on team strengths, and instituted weekly check-ins to track progress and address roadblocks. The results were remarkable: turnaround times improved by 22%, and his team's morale soared as they saw the benefits of clarity and collaboration. Inspired by James's newfound direction, the team adopted his methods, fostering a culture of accountability and shared success.

Both Emma and James demonstrated that setbacks and challenges are not the end—they're opportunities to innovate and improve. Emma turned a lost deal into a record-breaking quarter by leveraging her relationship-building skills and staying focused on her goals. Meanwhile, James transformed his team's productivity by adopting a structured approach and empowering his colleagues to work smarter. Together, their stories illustrate how resilience, strategic thinking, and clear goals can lead to exceptional achievements in any professional setting.

These examples offer valuable lessons: setbacks can spark innovation, and structure can transform chaos into success. Whether it's recovering from a major loss or streamlining workflows, the key lies in perseverance, adaptability, and a commitment to growth.

Conclusion: Take Charge of Your Goals

Effective goal setting transforms aspirations into actionable plans, while prioritization ensures those plans remain focused and achievable.

This week, challenge yourself to:

1. Set one professional SMART goal and one personal SMART goal.
2. Break each goal into smaller steps, assign deadlines, and track your progress.

Remember, the journey toward your goals isn't always linear, but each step forward brings you closer to success. As Henry David Thoreau said, "What you get by achieving your goals is not as important as what you become by achieving your goals."

WEEK 4 CHALLENGE
Effective Goal Setting and Prioritization

Visual Guide: SMART Goal Template

Goal Component	Your Goal
Specific	What exactly do you want to achieve?
Measurable	How will you measure success?
Achievable	Is this goal realistic given your resources?
Relevant	Does this align with your broader aspirations?
Time-bound	What is your deadline?

Checklist:

- Write 1 professional SMART goal.
- Break the goal into 3 actionable steps.
- Share your goal with a trusted colleague or friend.

MINDFUL MOTION: THE ART OF LIVING WELL

Balanced Nutrition and Meal Planning – Essentials for creating nutrient-dense, balanced meals.

Affirmation
I am what I eat.

Motivational Quote
"Good nutrition creates health in all areas of our existence. All parts are interconnected." - T. Colin Campbell

Creating nutrient-dense, balanced meals is key to maintaining overall health and energy levels. Here are some practical tips to help you build meals that are packed with the nutrients your body needs:

Include a Variety of Whole Foods

- Fruits and Vegetables: Are rich in vitamins, minerals, antioxidants, and fiber.
- Aim to fill half your plate with one, or a combination of colorful non-starchy like broccoli, cauliflower, cucumber, dark leafy greens, tomatoes, bell peppers, eggplant, carrots, cabbage, zucchini.
- Choose 2-3 servings of fresh fruit daily for between meal snacks or dessert. A serving is a small piece, or one cup berries, grapes, or melon.
- Lean Proteins: Provide essential amino acids that help with muscle repair, immune function, and more.

- Incorporate palm sized portion of lean proteins like poultry, fish, beef/pork loin, tofu, or ¼ plate of beans, lentils, or eggs.
- Healthy Fats: Support brain health, hormone production, and joint health.
- Add a small amount of healthy fats such as avocado, olive oil, nuts, seeds, and fatty fish (like salmon and mackerel).
- Whole Grains and Starchy Vegetables: Provide complex carbohydrates for sustained energy and are rich in fiber, which aids digestion.
- Opt for ¼ plate (no more than 1 cup maximum) of whole grains like quinoa, brown rice, whole wheat pasta, oats, whole wheat bread, whole wheat tortillas, corn tortillas; potatoes, corn, peas, or squash.

By combining these principles into your daily meal planning, you'll be able to create nutrient-dense, balanced meals that support long-term health and wellness.

WEEK 5

ACTIVE LISTENING
& EMPATHY

ACTIVE LISTENING AND EMPATHY

In the world of leadership, effective communication isn't just about speaking—it's about listening. Active listening and empathy form the foundation of meaningful relationships, fostering trust, collaboration, and a sense of belonging within teams. These skills go beyond merely hearing words; they require a leader to fully engage with others, understand their perspectives, and respond thoughtfully. Research from *The Center for Creative Leadership* highlights that 91% of employees view their managers' communication skills as critical to job satisfaction, underscoring the importance of these transformative tools.

Listening Beyond Words

Active listening involves more than just processing what is being said, it requires attentiveness to tone, body language, and unspoken emotions. A leader who practices active listening demonstrates a commitment to understanding their team's needs and concerns. This skill can significantly impact organizational outcomes. According to a *Harvard Business Review* study, managers who listen actively are 67% more likely to foster high levels of employee engagement. When employees feel heard, they are more motivated, creative, and aligned with organizational goals.

Consider Elena, a team leader at a high-pressure tech startup. Focused on meeting tight deadlines, she failed to recognize the signs of burnout within her team. It wasn't until a key team member resigned unexpectedly that she realized the consequences of her oversight. By adopting a new approach—engaging in active listening and demonstrating empathy—Elena rebuilt trust within her team. She began conducting regular check-ins, asking open-ended questions, and addressing concerns directly. Her efforts not only improved morale but also increased productivity and team cohesion, illustrating the power of listening to the challenges that lie beneath the surface.

The Role of Empathy

Empathy complements active listening by helping leaders connect on an emotional level. It allows them to see the world through their team members' eyes, fostering deeper understanding and compassion. Neuroscience research reveals that empathy activates mirror neurons in the brain, creating a sense of shared experience. In a workplace setting, this shared understanding can strengthen relationships and promote a culture of inclusion. A study from *Businessolver's State of Workplace Empathy Report* found that 90% of employees believe empathy is a key driver of workplace performance, yet only 50% feel their leaders consistently demonstrate it.

Practical Applications

Developing active listening and empathy requires intentionality and practice. Techniques such as maintaining eye contact, avoiding interruptions, and paraphrasing key points can help leaders improve their listening skills. Empathy can be cultivated by asking questions like, "How can I better support you?" or "What challenges are you facing, and how do they impact you?" These small actions signal genuine care and foster a sense of safety. Analytics show that empathetic leaders are 70% more likely to retain top talent, as employees are drawn to environments where they feel valued and understood.

Transforming Leadership Through Connection

Active listening and empathy are not just "soft skills"; they are strategic assets that drive team performance, innovation, and satisfaction. When leaders make a conscious effort to listen beyond words and empathize with their team's experiences, they create a ripple effect of trust and collaboration. This week, we'll explore actionable strategies to develop and apply these skills in real-world scenarios, empowering you to lead with understanding and connection. Leadership isn't just about decisions—it's about building bridges that inspire and sustain success.

What Is Active Listening?

Active listening is more than just hearing words—it's fully engaging in the conversation to understand the speaker's perspective and intent.

Key Differences Between Active Listening and Passive Hearing

- **Passive Hearing**: Simply absorbing sound without processing its meaning.
- **Active Listening**: Fully concentrating, understanding, and responding thoughtfully to what's being said.

Core Components of Active Listening

1. **Focus**: Give your full attention to the speaker.
2. **Reflection**: Paraphrase or summarize to confirm understanding.
3. **Response**: Ask clarifying questions and provide thoughtful feedback.

Example: During a client meeting, instead of nodding passively, a project manager summarized the client's concerns and asked, "Did I capture that correctly?" This ensured alignment and strengthened the client's trust.

Practical Techniques for Active Listening

1. Eliminate Distractions
- Put away your phone and avoid multitasking.
- Maintain steady eye contact to signal engagement.

2. Use Verbal and Non-Verbal Cues
- **Verbal**: "I see," "That's a good point," or "Can you elaborate on that?"

- **Non-Verbal**: Nod, smile, or lean forward slightly to show interest.

3. Paraphrase and Clarify

Restating the speaker's message in your own words ensures you understand correctly. For example:
- Speaker: "I'm overwhelmed by the new project scope."
- Listener: "It sounds like the expanded scope is adding pressure. Is that right?"

4. Recognize Non-Verbal Cues
- Pay attention to body language, tone, and facial expressions.
- If someone's tone contradicts their words, address it gently: "You're saying it's fine, but you seem a bit concerned—can we discuss this further?"

Empathy: The Bridge to Understanding

Empathy is the ability to understand and share another person's feelings, even if you don't fully agree with their perspective. In the workplace, empathy can:

- Strengthen relationships.
- Improve collaboration.
- Resolve conflicts effectively.

Why Empathy Matters

Empathy goes beyond sympathy (feeling sorry for someone). It's about actively trying to see the world through their eyes.

Example: A frustrated employee might say, "I feel like my work isn't valued." An empathetic leader responds, "I understand how that could feel discouraging. Let's talk about how we can recognize your contributions better."

Building Empathy in Communication

1. Practice Perspective-Taking
Ask yourself:
- "How would I feel in their position?"
- "What factors might be influencing their behavior?"

2. Recognize Emotional Cues
- Observe tone, expressions, and pacing for emotional context.
- Use statements like, "It seems like you're feeling frustrated. Is that right?"

3. Respond with Compassion, Not Solutions
Often, people don't need you to "fix" their problems; they just need to feel heard. Instead of jumping to solutions, try:
- "That sounds really challenging. How can I support you?"

4. Balance Empathy with Boundaries
While empathy is crucial, it's important to maintain professional boundaries. For example:
- Acknowledge emotions without overcommitting: "I understand you're feeling overwhelmed. Let's see what adjustments we can make to help."

STORY

From Setbacks to Transformative Leadership

Nathan, a no-nonsense department head, and Emma, a results-driven sales director, both faced challenges that tested their leadership skills and emotional intelligence. While their situations differed, their ability to adapt, listen, and act strategically transformed not only their outcomes but also their relationships with their teams.

Nathan was accustomed to running a tight ship, setting high expectations, and expecting his team to deliver. However, when his team began consistently missing deadlines, he grew frustrated, assuming they were slacking off. Determined to address the issue, he called a team meeting. Initially, his direct approach dominated the conversation, but he noticed Claire, a senior team member, hesitating to speak. Instead of moving forward with his assumptions, Nathan paused and said, "Claire, I'd really like to hear your perspective."

Claire hesitated but eventually shared that the team was struggling with unclear priorities and growing burnout. For the first time, Nathan truly listened. He paraphrased Claire's concerns to ensure he understood, thanked her for her honesty, and opened the floor for more input. Over the next few weeks, Nathan held one-on-one meetings with each team member to gather deeper insights. This empathetic approach revealed systemic issues in workflow management and communication. In response, Nathan restructured workloads, prioritized tasks more clearly, and implemented regular check-ins to maintain alignment. Within three months, deadlines were consistently met, and the team reported a 30% improvement in morale. Nathan, once seen as a taskmaster, gained a reputation as a trusted and compassionate leader.

Emma's challenge, while different, also required resilience and a shift in approach. As a sales director, she was devastated when a high-profile client deal fell through. It was a significant financial and emotional blow, but Emma refused to let the loss define her. Drawing on her relationship-building skills, she identified five promising prospects in her pipeline and dedicated herself to strengthening those connections. She personalized her outreach, conducted in-depth research to align her pitches with client needs, and followed up diligently.

The result was extraordinary. Within a single quarter, Emma not only recovered the lost revenue but exceeded her targets by 25%. Her proactive approach earned her recognition from company leadership, and her ability to turn a setback into an opportunity became a case study within her department.

Nathan and Emma's stories underscore the power of resilience, empathy, and adaptability in leadership. Nathan's willingness to listen transformed his team's performance, while Emma's determination to

refocus turned a major setback into an achievement. Together, their experiences illustrate that great leadership is not about avoiding challenges—it's about facing them head-on with empathy, strategy, and an unwavering commitment to growth.

These examples highlight key takeaways: listening can uncover hidden issues, resilience turns failure into opportunity, and effective leadership requires both emotional intelligence and strategic action. In every challenge lies the potential for transformation, and leaders like Nathan and Emma show that success is built not just on results, but on the trust, engagement, and motivation they inspire in others.

Listen, Understand, Act

Active listening and empathy aren't innate traits—they are skills you can develop with practice. This week, challenge yourself to:

1. Fully engage in one conversation each day.
2. Use paraphrasing and clarifying questions to confirm understanding.
3. Reflect on how empathy can improve your workplace relationships.

By mastering these skills, you'll become a communicator who inspires trust, builds deeper connections, and fosters collaboration. Remember, listening and empathy aren't just about hearing words—they're about understanding the people behind them.

WEEK 5 CHALLENGE
Active Listening and Empathy

Visual Guide: 3 Steps of Active Listening

Step	What to Do
Focus	Eliminate distractions and maintain eye contact.
Reflect	Paraphrase what the speaker says to confirm understanding.
Respond	Ask clarifying questions and provide thoughtful replies.

Checklist:

- Choose one daily conversation to practice active listening.
- Paraphrase at least one statement in each conversation.
- Note how active listening impacts the interaction.

MINDFUL MOTION:
THE ART OF LIVING WELL

**Fuel your Workout – The importance of fueling
and hydrating before, during, and after exercise**

Affirmation:
I set myself up for success by nourishing my body to get the most
out of my workout.

Motivational Quote:
"Eating healthy food fills your body with energy and nutrients. Imagine your cells smiling back at you and saying: 'Thank
you!'" – Karen Salmansohn

To maximize performance and ensure optimal results from your
workouts, proper fueling and hydration are crucial. The body
relies on a balanced intake of carbohydrates, proteins, fats, and
adequate hydration to support exercise, recovery, and overall
health. Since the human body is composed of about 60% water,
even a small decrease in hydration levels (as little as 2-3% of body
weight) can negatively impact performance. Therefore, maintaining the right balance of nutrition and fluid intake before,
during, and after exercise is key to enhancing your training and
performance.

Pre-Exercise Fueling and Hydration

3-4 Hours Before Exercise:
- **Fuel:** Consume a well-balanced meal that includes a good
  portion of carbohydrates, moderate protein, and low fat.

Carbs are the body's primary energy source during exercise, so foods like whole grains (brown rice, whole wheat pasta, oatmeal), starchy vegetables (sweet potatoes, potatoes, corn), and fruits (bananas, apples, strawberries) should make up a large part of your meal. Include lean proteins like chicken, fish, eggs, or nuts to help keep hunger at bay during your workout. Avoid excessive fats and fiber, as they can lead to digestive discomfort during exercise.

- **Hydrate:** Stay hydrated by sipping water throughout the day, especially in the hours leading up to your workout. Be sure to drink water, milk, or 100% fruit juice to keep your body properly hydrated.

30-60 Minutes Before Exercise:
- **Fuel:** Have a small, carbohydrate-rich snack to boost your energy levels just before you start exercising. Examples include a piece of fruit or a granola bar.
- **Hydrate:** Drink approximately 8-20 oz. of fluid to ensure your body is well-hydrated and ready for the activity ahead.

During Exercise Fueling and Hydration

For Exercises Under 60 Minutes:
- **Fuel:** For shorter workouts, fueling during the session may not be necessary unless you are feeling fatigued. Water should be sufficient for hydration.
- **Hydrate:** Water is typically the best option for staying hydrated during brief exercise sessions.

For Exercises Over 60 Minutes:

- **Fuel:** For longer sessions, it's beneficial to have a carbohydrate-rich snack to maintain energy levels. This could include a banana, energy bar, or other easily digestible carbohydrate sources.
- **Hydrate:** Sports drinks can be a good option during longer workouts, as they provide both hydration and help replenish electrolytes lost through sweat. Aim to drink 4-6 oz. of fluid every 15 minutes during extended exercise sessions.

For Tournaments or Multi-Event Days:

- **Fuel:** Plan ahead by packing snacks and easy-to-carry meals. Stick to foods you are familiar with to avoid stomach upset during competition.
- **Hydrate:** Take advantage of breaks during the event to rehydrate with water or sports drinks to maintain optimal hydration levels.

Post-Exercise Fueling and Hydration

Within 15-60 Minutes After Exercise:

- **Fuel:** After exercising, your body needs carbohydrates to replenish glycogen stores and protein to support muscle recovery. A snack or meal that combines both carbs and protein is ideal, such as a smoothie with fruit and protein powder, or a sandwich with lean protein and whole grains.
- **Hydrate:** Rehydrate by drinking 16-24 oz. of water for every pound of body weight lost through sweat. This helps your body return to its optimal temperature and reestablish fluid balance.

2-3 Hours After Exercise:

- **Fuel:** Eat a well-rounded meal with a balance of carbohydrates, protein, and fats to continue the recovery process. This helps restore energy and support muscle repair.
- **Hydrate:** Continue drinking fluids and include water-rich foods like fruits and vegetables in your post-workout meals to further support hydration.

Remember that you cannot out-train poor nutrition or hydration. Proper fueling and hydration are just as important as your workout routine itself. By making sure you provide your body with the nutrients and fluids it needs before, during, and after exercise, you ensure that your muscles recover properly, your energy levels remain high, and your overall performance is optimized. Make food and hydration a priority to fuel your body for success!

WEEK 6

GIVING AND
RECEIVING FEEDBACK
Feedback as a Growth Catalyst

GIVING AND RECEIVING FEEDBACK

Feedback as a Growth Catalyst

Feedback is the compass that guides improvement. Whether it's praise for a job well done or constructive advice for better performance, feedback is a crucial driver of personal and professional growth. Yet, many people dread it—either because they fear receiving it or struggle to give it effectively.

Consider Emma, a product designer who struggled with receiving feedback early in her career. She often viewed critiques as personal attacks, which caused tension with her team. Over time, Emma learned to reframe feedback as an opportunity for growth. By adopting a proactive approach, she transformed her work and relationships, earning recognition for her ability to adapt and improve.

This week, we'll explore how to give feedback that inspires action and receive feedback with grace and a growth mindset.

The Art of Giving Feedback

Delivering feedback effectively is as much about how you say it as what you say.

Characteristics of Effective Feedback

1. **Timely**: Provide feedback as close to the event as possible. Delayed feedback often loses its relevance.
2. **Specific**: Vague comments like "You need to improve" don't help. Focus on particular behaviors or outcomes.
3. **Actionable**: Suggest clear, practical steps for improvement.

Frameworks for Delivering Feedback

One useful framework is the **SBI Model**:

- **Situation**: Describe the context.
- **Behavior**: Identify the specific behavior.
- **Impact**: Explain the effect of that behavior.

Example: Instead of saying, "Your presentation was confusing," try:

- "During the team meeting (situation), your slides lacked a clear summary (behavior), which made it hard for the team to understand next steps (impact)."

Avoiding Common Pitfalls

- **Focusing on Personality**: Critique actions, not character. Replace "You're disorganized" with "The deadlines were missed because the timeline wasn't clear."
- **Overloading Feedback**: Address one or two key issues instead of overwhelming the recipient with multiple critiques.

The Skill of Receiving Feedback

Receiving feedback, especially constructive criticism, can feel challenging. However, adopting the right mindset can transform these moments into growth opportunities.

Reframing Feedback

- See feedback as a gift—it's information that can help you grow.
- Understand that feedback isn't about your worth; it's about your actions or performance.

Techniques for Constructive Responses

1. **Stay Calm**: Pause, breathe, and avoid defensiveness.
2. **Listen Actively**: Resist the urge to interrupt or explain yourself.
3. **Clarify**: Ask questions like, "Can you give me an example?" or "What would improvement look like?"

Turning Feedback into Action

- Reflect on the feedback: What resonates? What can you improve?
- Create a plan to address the feedback and check back with the giver to demonstrate progress.

STORY

From Miscommunication to Masterful Leadership

Alex, a dedicated team lead, and Nathan, a no-nonsense department head, both faced challenges that pushed them to reevaluate their approaches to leadership and communication. Through feedback, reflection, and decisive action, they turned obstacles into opportunities for growth, transforming their teams and their own leadership styles.

Alex had always prided himself on being an effective communicator. So when a colleague shared feedback that his emails were often unclear and caused confusion, he initially felt offended and defensive. He thought, *I'm doing my best to stay concise—how is this a problem?* However, after taking some time to reflect, he realized that dismissing the feedback wouldn't solve the issue. Determined to improve, Alex reached out to a trusted colleague for advice. Together, they reviewed examples of his emails, and Alex began to see the problem: his brevity sometimes omitted crucial context or left room for misinterpretation.

Taking the feedback to heart, Alex worked on crafting clearer, more structured messages. He adopted techniques like starting with a summary, outlining key points with bullet lists, and ensuring each email ended with clear action items. Within weeks, the results were noticeable. Team members no longer emailed back for clarification, and meetings became more productive because everyone arrived prepared and aligned. Over the next quarter, misunderstandings decreased by 40%, and his team's productivity saw a measurable boost. Alex's willingness to embrace feedback not only improved communication but also reinforced trust and cohesion within his team.

Nathan, on the other hand, faced a larger-scale challenge. As a department head, he was known for his high expectations and no-nonsense approach. When his team started missing deadlines, Nathan assumed the problem was a lack of effort. Frustrated, he called a meeting to address the issue head-on. However, during the meeting, he noticed Claire, a senior team member, hesitating to speak. Pausing his usual directive style, Nathan said, "Claire, I'd really like to hear your perspective."

Claire's response opened his eyes to the real problem: unclear priorities and mounting burnout were overwhelming the team. Recognizing the need for a change, Nathan committed to listening more actively. He held one-on-one meetings with each team member, gathering valuable insights about workflow bottlenecks and communication gaps. Nathan used this feedback to streamline task prioritization, clarify expectations, and implement weekly check-ins to maintain alignment.

Within three months, the impact was clear. Deadlines were met consistently, and team morale improved by 30%. Nathan's willingness to shift from a directive to an empathetic leadership style earned him not only his team's trust but also their renewed enthusiasm for their work.

Both Alex and Nathan demonstrate that feedback, even when difficult to hear, is a powerful catalyst for growth. Alex turned a small but critical insight into a game-changing improvement in communication, while Nathan transformed his leadership approach to build a more cohesive and motivated team. Their stories highlight the importance of listening, adapting, and taking deliberate steps to create a culture of clarity, trust, and collaboration.

These examples also underscore a valuable lesson: effective leadership isn't about being perfect—it's about being open to learning and evolving. Whether it's refining communication or creating space for team input, leaders who embrace growth inspire not only better results but also stronger connections with their teams. In doing so, they lay the foundation for long-term success and shared achievements.

Creating a Feedback Culture

Feedback is more than just a one-off exchange between a manager and an employee—it's the foundation of trust, collaboration, and continuous improvement in high-performing teams and organizations. When embedded into the culture of a workplace, feedback transforms from a potentially uncomfortable conversation into a powerful tool for growth and innovation.

Encouraging Open Communication

Building a culture of feedback starts with creating an environment where open communication is valued and encouraged. Leaders play a crucial role in setting the tone by modeling openness themselves. When leaders actively seek feedback—whether it's on their leadership style, decision-making, or organizational strategies—they demonstrate that feedback is not a critique but an opportunity for growth. For instance, a leader might regularly ask their team, "How can I better support you in achieving your goals?" This signals vulnerability and a willingness to improve, paving the way for others to do the same.

Equally important is reducing the fear often associated with giving or receiving feedback. Employees need reassurance that feedback is not about assigning blame or punishment but about fostering development and addressing challenges constructively. Leaders can emphasize this by framing feedback as a shared journey toward achieving team goals, making it clear that everyone has a role in driving improvement.

Making Feedback Routine

Feedback should not be reserved for annual performance reviews—it needs to be a regular part of team dynamics. Incorporating feedback sessions into team meetings, one-on-ones, or project retrospectives normalizes the practice and ensures continuous dialogue. For example, dedicating the last five minutes of a weekly meeting to questions like "What's one thing we can do better next week?" encourages reflection and promotes incremental improvements.

Leveraging structured tools, such as 360-degree feedback, can also enhance the process by providing diverse perspectives. This approach ensures that feedback isn't limited to top-down interactions but flows across all levels of the organization, fostering a culture of mutual respect and shared accountability. Tools like anonymous surveys or feedback apps can further encourage honest input, especially from team members who might hesitate to speak up directly.

STORY

Building a Feedback Habit

At a mid-sized company, a forward-thinking manager implemented a simple but transformative practice. At the start of every team meeting, she would ask, "What's one thing we can improve as a team?" Initially, the responses were surface level, as team members were cautious about speaking up. But over time, as the manager consistently acknowledged and acted on their suggestions, the team began to embrace the process.

This practice normalized feedback, empowering team members to voice ideas and concerns without fear of judgment. The results were tangible: employee satisfaction scores improved by 20%, and the team's productivity increased as bottlenecks and inefficiencies were addressed promptly. This example demonstrates how consistent, open feedback practices can lead to a more engaged, innovative, and high-performing team.

Building a Feedback-Driven Organization

Creating a feedback culture requires commitment, but the payoff is significant. When employees feel heard and valued, they are more likely to engage, collaborate, and contribute to the organization's success. Feedback not only drives personal and professional growth but also strengthens trust and alignment across teams. By embedding feedback into daily routines and fostering an environment of openness, organizations can unlock their full potential and empower everyone to thrive.

S T O R Y

Transforming Through Feedback

Sophia, a junior marketing associate at a mid-sized tech company, was enthusiastic about her work but deeply apprehensive about feedback. During her first major project, she presented a campaign proposal to senior leaders with high hopes. However, the response was not what she anticipated. Her approach, while creative, didn't align with the company's established brand voice. The feedback, delivered constructively but directly, left Sophia feeling embarrassed and defensive. She worried that her ideas—and her capabilities—were being dismissed.

After an initial wave of self-doubt, Sophia realized this was an opportunity to grow. Instead of shutting down, she decided to approach her manager for clarity. "Could you help me understand how I can align my work better with the brand's voice?" she asked.

Her manager appreciated her willingness to learn and provided concrete examples of past campaigns that resonated with the company's target audience. With this guidance, Sophia revisited her proposal, analyzing her content through the lens of the feedback she had received.

The transformation was remarkable. Sophia's revised campaign not only aligned with the company's brand voice but also introduced innovative elements that elevated its appeal. When she presented it again, the senior leaders praised her for her creativity and strategic alignment. The campaign was approved and went on to exceed expectations, boosting engagement metrics by 35% compared to the company's previous efforts.

This experience was a turning point for Sophia. She discovered that feedback, while sometimes uncomfortable, is a powerful tool for growth when approached with curiosity and openness. Embracing feedback became part of her professional philosophy. Over the next two years, she applied the same mindset to every project, seeking input early and often. Her adaptability and proactive approach earned her a reputation as a reliable and innovative marketer.

By the time Sophia was promoted to lead high-profile campaigns, her leadership reflected the lessons she had learned through feedback. She created an environment where her team felt safe to give and receive constructive input, fostering collaboration and continuous improvement. Under her leadership, the team launched a global campaign that increased brand recognition by 50% and drove a 20% increase in sales within the first quarter.

Sophia's journey underscores a vital lesson: feedback is not a judgment of your worth but an opportunity to refine your skills and achieve excellence. By embracing feedback with a growth mindset, you can turn challenges into steppingstones, build stronger professional relationships, and unlock your true potential.

Conclusion: Feedback as a Two-Way Street

Giving and receiving feedback are skills that require practice and intentionality. To grow personally and professionally, embrace feedback as a tool, not a threat.

This week, challenge yourself to:

1. Give constructive feedback using the SBI framework.
2. Ask someone for feedback on an area you want to improve.

By fostering a culture of open, constructive feedback, you'll build stronger relationships and accelerate your growth. Remember, feedback isn't just about pointing out what's wrong—it's about helping each other become the best versions of ourselves.

WEEK 6 CHALLENGE
Giving and Receiving Feedback

Visual Guide: Feedback Cycle

Phase	What to Focus On
Giving Feedback	Use the SBI model: Situation, Behavior, Impact.
Receiving Feedback	Ask clarifying questions and listen actively.
Actioning Feedback	Write down key takeaways and set improvement goals.

Checklist:

- Deliver feedback using the SBI model.
- Seek feedback on one specific skill or behavior.
- Act on the feedback and track your progress.

MINDFUL MOTION: THE ART OF LIVING WELL

Keep the Carbs

Affirmation:

I will fuel my body efficiently.

Motivational Quote:

"Sorry, there's no magic bullet. You gotta eat healthy and live healthy to be healthy and look healthy. End of story." – Morgan Spurlock, documentarian, film maker, and producer

Carbohydrates are an essential part of a healthy diet for several important reasons. While they sometimes get a bad reputation, especially with certain diet trends, carbs are a crucial source of energy and play several key roles in maintaining overall health. Here's why it's important to keep carbohydrates in your diet:

Primary Source of Energy - Carbohydrates are the body's preferred source of energy. When you consume carbs, your body breaks them down into glucose, which is used by your cells, tissues, and organs for energy. This energy is especially important for fueling your brain, muscles, and other vital functions throughout the day. Your diet should contain 45% - 65% carbohydrates.

- **Brain Function** - The brain relies on glucose as its primary fuel. Low carbohydrate intake can lead to low blood sugar levels, which may affect your ability to focus, concentrate and think clearly.

- **Supports Physical Activity** - Carbohydrates are essential for athletes and active individuals because they provide the quick energy needed during physical activity. Helping you perform better and recover more efficiently.
- **Digestive Health** - Complex carbohydrates, especially those found in whole grains, vegetables, and legumes, are high in fiber. Fiber aids digestion by promoting regular bowel movements, preventing constipation, and supporting a healthy gut microbiome. Fiber also helps regulate blood sugar levels and lowers the risk of chronic conditions like type 2 diabetes and heart disease.
- **Helps with Satiety** - Carbohydrates, especially those high in fiber, help you feel fuller for longer. This can prevent overeating and help manage hunger between meals, balance your appetite and support weight management.

Carbohydrates, particularly from whole food sources, are a vital part of a balanced diet. They provide energy, support brain and muscle function, help regulate digestion, blood sugar, and provide essential nutrients. Rather than cutting carbs entirely, focusing on choosing healthy, nutrient-dense sources of carbohydrates promote overall health and well-being.

WEEK 7

MANAGING UP
& SUPPORTING
LEADERSHIP

MANAGING UP AND SUPPORTING LEADERSHIP

Leadership in its most effective form is a two-way street. While leaders are tasked with setting direction and supporting their teams, employees also play a vital role in fostering collaboration by managing up. Managing up is the art of understanding your leader's goals, priorities, and work style to proactively support them. This approach not only strengthens relationships but also enhances team efficiency and fosters mutual respect. In today's dynamic workplace, employees who manage up contribute to a culture of alignment and shared success.

What is Managing Up?

Managing up goes beyond merely following orders; it's about taking initiative and ensuring that you and your leader are on the same page. Research from *Harvard Business Review* highlights that employees who effectively manage up are 33% more likely to report job satisfaction and career advancement. By understanding your leader's communication style, anticipating their needs, and delivering on expectations, you create a partnership that benefits both parties. Managing up also involves providing solutions rather than just presenting problems, making you an indispensable asset to your team.

Consider Daniel, a mid-level analyst who struggled with unclear expectations and missed deadlines. His relationship with his manager was strained, and performance reviews reflected a lack of alignment. Recognizing the need for change, Daniel began practicing managing up. He started by learning his manager's top priorities, preferred communication methods, and decision-making processes. By adapting his approach and proactively addressing potential issues, Daniel improved their working relationship, resulting in clearer communication, timely deliverables, and glowing performance reviews. His story underscores the power of managing up to bridge gaps and build trust.

Why Managing Up Matters

Analytics show that organizations with strong employee-leader alignment experience 21% higher productivity, according to *Gallup's State of the Global Workplace* report. Managing up fosters this alignment by ensuring that employees are not only meeting expectations but also anticipating ways to add value. When employees take the time to understand their leaders' goals, they can prioritize tasks more effectively, reducing inefficiencies and misunderstandings. Moreover, managing up builds a foundation of trust, as leaders feel supported, and employees are empowered to take ownership of their roles.

Practical Strategies for Managing Up

1. Clarify Expectations: Schedule regular check-ins to align on goals and deadlines. Ask questions like, "What are the top priorities for this week?" or "How can I best support you?"
2. Adapt to Their Style: Pay attention to your leader's preferred methods of communication. If they value concise updates, tailor your emails and conversations accordingly.
3. Be Proactive: Anticipate challenges and propose solutions before they arise. For example, if a deadline might be missed, suggest a realistic adjustment and outline steps to stay on track.
4. Provide Feedback Thoughtfully: Managing up doesn't mean blindly following orders. If you see a better way to achieve a goal, share your perspective in a constructive manner that respects their leadership.

The Benefits of Managing Up

By mastering the art of managing up, you not only improve your relationship with your leader but also position yourself as a proactive and indispensable team member. This approach leads to enhanced career opportunities, as employees who actively support their leaders are often considered for promotions and greater responsibilities. *Forbes* notes that professionals who excel at managing up are 50% more likely to be identified as high-potential employees.

A Partnership for Success

Managing up is a skill that benefits both employees and leaders, creating a more collaborative and productive workplace. It transforms the traditional top-down dynamic into a partnership where both parties work toward shared success. This week, we'll delve deeper into the techniques for managing up, exploring real-world examples and actionable strategies that can help you enhance your professional relationships and accelerate your career trajectory. Leadership isn't just about following—it's about contributing to a vision and thriving together.

Understanding Your Leader's Style and Goals

No two leaders are alike. To manage up effectively, you must first understand your leader's unique style and objectives.

Identifying Leadership Styles

- **The Big Picture Thinker**: Prefers high-level summaries and future-focused discussions.
- **The Detail-Oriented Leader**: Appreciates thoroughness and regular updates.
- **The Collaborative Leader**: Values input and brainstorming from the team.

Aligning with Their Goals

Once you understand their style, align your work with their strategic objectives. Ask yourself:

- What are their top priorities?
- How does my role contribute to these goals?

Example: When Priya noticed her manager's emphasis on client satisfaction, she proactively included client feedback summaries in her project updates, earning praise for her initiative.

Proactive Communication

Effective communication is at the heart of managing up. It's about providing the right information at the right time.

Keeping Leaders Informed

- **Summarize Key Updates**: Instead of lengthy reports, provide concise summaries.
- **Offer Context**: Share background information to help leaders make informed decisions.

Anticipating Needs

- Think ahead about what your leader might require. For example, if a quarterly review is approaching, prepare performance data in advance.
- Offer solutions alongside problems: "I noticed an issue with X, and here's a potential way to resolve it."

STORY

Alex's Proactive Approach Leads to Success

Alex, a sales coordinator at a growing logistics firm, was known for his dedication and efficiency in managing client accounts. However, he wanted to stand out and demonstrate his potential for leadership roles. One day, as he reviewed the company's sales metrics, he noticed a pattern: while new client acquisition was strong, retention rates for existing clients were declining. Alex realized this could be a critical issue for the company's long-term growth, so he decided to take initiative.

Without being prompted, Alex began compiling a detailed client retention analysis. He pulled data from customer feedback surveys, analyzed purchasing trends over the last two years, and identified common reasons why clients discontinued their services. For example, his analysis revealed that 45% of clients who left cited inconsistent follow-ups from account managers, while another 30% pointed to a lack of personalized communication.

Alex didn't stop at identifying problems; he also proposed solutions. He outlined a retention strategy that included creating automated follow-up schedules for account managers, launching a quarterly client appreciation program, and segmenting clients for more personalized outreach. To make his case compelling, Alex included a projected 15% increase in client retention rates over six months if his recommendations were implemented, backed by industry benchmarks and case studies.

When Alex presented his analysis during the team's monthly meeting, his manager was not only impressed but also inspired by his initiative. The presentation sparked a discussion among senior leaders, leading to the implementation of several of Alex's recommendations. Within six months, the company saw a 12% improvement in client retention, with positive feedback from long-term customers about the personalized communication efforts.

Alex's proactive approach didn't go unnoticed. His manager recognized his ability to think strategically and solve problems before they escalated. As a result, Alex was entrusted with greater responsibilities, including leading a cross-functional team to develop a comprehensive client relationship management (CRM) system. His leadership in this project further solidified his reputation as a forward-thinking and dependable team member.

By taking initiative and addressing challenges without waiting to be asked, Alex demonstrated the value of proactive problem-solving in driving both personal and organizational success. His story highlights a critical lesson for professionals: anticipating needs, presenting data-driven solutions, and taking ownership of challenges can set you apart and pave the way for career growth. Through his actions, Alex not only earned the trust of his manager but also contributed to the company's bottom line, reinforcing the importance of initiative in the workplace.

Balancing Assertiveness with Respect

Managing up isn't about saying yes to everything—it's about finding the right balance between assertiveness and respect.

Confidently Expressing Ideas

- Frame suggestions around organizational goals: "I believe this approach aligns with our objective to increase efficiency."
- Use data to support your points. Leaders value evidence-based recommendations.

Respecting Boundaries

- Avoid overstepping or challenging decisions aggressively. Instead, ask questions to understand their perspective: "Can you share more about why this approach is preferred?"

Example: Jenna, a marketing strategist, respectfully voiced her concerns about a campaign's timeline. By presenting alternative solutions, she earned her manager's respect and contributed to a more successful launch.

The Benefits of Managing Up

When you support leadership effectively, you reap benefits that extend beyond workplace harmony.

Building Trust and Credibility

- Consistent communication and proactive behavior build trust over time.
- Leaders are more likely to rely on you for critical tasks.

Gaining Autonomy

- When leaders trust your judgment, you'll enjoy greater independence in decision-making.
- This autonomy fosters skill development and professional growth.

Example: Over a year, Robert, an operations associate, became his manager's go-to person for process improvements. By aligning his work with the department's goals, he earned a promotion to a supervisory role.

STORY

Turning Challenges into Opportunities

Carmen, a skilled account manager at a fast-paced marketing agency, found herself at a crossroads when her team got a new boss. Her manager, Mark, had a reputation for being extremely detail-oriented, with a penchant for frequent check-ins and an expectation for granular data at every turn. For Carmen, who thrived on autonomy and big-picture thinking, this new dynamic felt stifling and frustrating. She often felt like her independence was being micromanaged, and her productivity initially took a hit.

However, Carmen was determined to make the relationship work. Rather than resist, she decided to adapt. She began by studying Mark's previous projects and reports, noting the level of detail and structure he valued. From this, she realized that Mark's meticulous approach stemmed from a desire for precision and accountability, not a lack of trust. Armed with this understanding, Carmen took proactive steps to align her work style with his expectations.

First, she introduced detailed weekly reports summarizing key metrics, project updates, and next steps. These reports not only addressed Mark's need for data but also reduced the need for last-minute requests. Next, she scheduled regular one-on-one meetings to anticipate and address questions before they became issues. By preparing for these discussions in advance, Carmen demonstrated her commitment to meeting Mark's standards and took control of their interactions.

The changes paid off. Over the next few months, Carmen noticed a significant shift in their working relationship. Mark began trusting her judgment, delegating critical projects with minimal oversight. For instance, when the agency landed a major client, Mark assigned Carmen to lead the account independently. Her ability to handle the responsibility without constant input proved to Mark that she was not only capable but also aligned with his vision.

Carmen's efforts didn't just improve her rapport with Mark—they also enhanced her own leadership skills. By managing up, she learned how to navigate different management styles, a crucial skill in any workplace. Furthermore, her proactive approach fostered a culture of transparency within her team,

making them more efficient and cohesive. Within a year, Carmen was promoted to senior account manager, leading a team and applying the lessons she'd learned to mentor others.

This experience taught Carmen the importance of adaptability and proactive communication in turning challenges into opportunities. Her story highlights that difficult working relationships don't have to be roadblocks—they can be catalysts for personal and professional growth. By stepping out of her comfort zone, Carmen not only strengthened her connection with her boss but also set herself up for long-term success, proving that with the right mindset, even the toughest challenges can lead to transformative opportunities.

Conclusion: A Win-Win Approach

Managing up is about creating a mutually beneficial relationship between you and your leader. By understanding their goals, communicating proactively, and balancing assertiveness with respect, you can build trust and contribute more effectively.

Challenge yourself this week to:

1. Observe your leader's style and identify one way to align your work with their priorities.
2. Offer a solution to a problem before being asked.

Remember, managing up isn't about flattery or self-promotion—it's about fostering collaboration and making your workplace thrive.

WEEK 7 CHALLENGE
Giving and Receiving Feedback

Visual Guide: Feedback Cycle

Phase	What to Focus On
Giving Feedback	Use the SBI model: Situation, Behavior, Impact.
Receiving Feedback	Ask clarifying questions and listen actively.
Actioning Feedback	Write down key takeaways and set improvement goals.

Checklist:

- Deliver feedback using the SBI model.
- Seek feedback on one specific skill or behavior.
- Act on the feedback and track your progress.

MINDFUL MOTION:
THE ART OF LIVING WELL

Bone and Joint Health

Affirmation
I am strong.

Motivational Quote
"Today is your day to start fresh, to eat right, to train hard, to live healthy, to be proud." – Bonnie Pfiester

Importance of strength training, calcium, and vitamin D for strong bones.

Maintaining strong bones and joints is essential for overall health and mobility. As we age, the risk of bone-related issues such as osteoporosis and arthritis increases, making it crucial to focus on bone health from an early age. Strength training, calcium, and vitamin D play pivotal roles in ensuring the bones remain strong and resilient throughout life.

Strength training, also known as resistance or weight-bearing exercise, involves lifting weights or performing activities that work muscles against resistance. This type of exercise is not only beneficial for building muscle but is also crucial for maintaining healthy bones.

- **Bone Density:** Bone density declines after the age of 30. Regular strength training 2-3 days per week, helps stimulate bone-forming cells called osteoblasts, promoting increased bone density and strength.

- **Joint Health:** Strength training also supports joint health by strengthening the muscles and ligaments that surround the joints, providing better support and reducing the risk of joint injuries.
- **Preventing Osteoporosis:** Osteoporosis is a condition characterized by weakened bones that are more prone to fractures. Regular weight-bearing exercises, such as squats, lunges, and resistance training, can help maintain or even increase bone density, lowering the risk of osteoporosis as we age.
- **Calcium and Vitamin D:** Calcium and vitamin D work together in a complementary manner to support optimal bone health. Without adequate vitamin D, the calcium you consume will not be absorbed effectively, and your bones will not be able to fully benefit from the calcium that is available. Conversely, adequate calcium intake is important for fully realizing the benefits of vitamin D in promoting bone strength.
  - Calcium Recommendations:
  - Adults (19-50 years): 1,000 mg per day
  - Women (51+ years) and Men (71+ years): 1,200 mg per day

Sources of Calcium:

- Dairy products like milk, cheese, and yogurt
- Leafy green vegetables such as kale, collard greens, and broccoli; fortified plant-based milk (soy, almond, oat).
- Fish with edible bones, such as sardines and salmon; tofu, almonds, and fortified cereals.
- Vitamin D Recommendations:

- Adults (19-70 years): 600 IU (International Units) per day
- Adults (71+ years): 800 IU per day

Sources of Vitamin D:

- Sunlight - The body can produce vitamin D when the skin is exposed to sunlight. About 10 to 30 minutes of sun exposure several times a week (depending on skin tone, location, and weather) can generate adequate amounts of vitamin D.
- Diet - Some foods contain vitamin D naturally, including fatty fish (salmon, mackerel, tuna), egg yolks, and beef liver. Many foods, such as milk, orange juice, and breakfast cereals, are fortified with vitamin D.
- Supplements - In cases where it is difficult to get enough vitamin D from sunlight or food, supplements may be necessary. Vitamin D2 and vitamin D3 are both commonly used in supplements, with vitamin D3 being the more potent form
  - It's important to talk with a healthcare provider to assess your specific needs, as individual requirements can vary based on factors like health conditions, lifestyle, and geographic location.

*Aim for 2-3 servings of calcium rich foods, and 1 serving of vitamin D rich food + 1 serving fortified foods like milk, juice, cereal. Pairing calcium and vitamin D-rich foods together in one meal can maximize absorption. For example, you might have fortified cereal with plant-based milk (fortified with both calcium and vitamin D) or grilled salmon with a side of broccoli (calcium-rich) for dinner.

Weekly Journal Notes

Journal writing can be a powerful tool for self-reflection and personal growth. To get the most out of your journaling practice, set aside a specific time each day to write, creating a routine that fits your schedule. Start with a clear intention or prompt to guide your thoughts and write honestly without self-editing or judgment. Focus on your experiences, feelings, and insights, exploring both positive and challenging aspects of your day.

_____

_____

_____

_____

_____

_____

_____

_____

_____

_____

_____

WEEK 8

Resilience & Adaptability

WEEK 8

RESILIENCE AND ADAPTABILITY

In a world characterized by rapid change and uncertainty, resilience and adaptability have become essential skills for both personal and professional success. Life and work rarely go according to plan—markets fluctuate, teams reorganize, and unforeseen events can disrupt even the most carefully crafted strategies. However, individuals who cultivate resilience and adaptability do more than survive—they thrive. These qualities allow people to navigate challenges with confidence, seize new opportunities, and emerge stronger from adversity.

The Power of Resilience and Adaptability

Resilience is the ability to bounce back from setbacks, while adaptability is the capacity to adjust to new conditions. Together, they form the backbone of a growth mindset, enabling individuals to maintain focus and flexibility even in the face of unexpected obstacles. Research from the *American Psychological Association* shows that resilient individuals experience 26% lower stress levels and are 31% more likely to report job satisfaction compared to their less-resilient counterparts. Adaptability, meanwhile, has been linked to increased innovation and problem-solving capabilities.

According to a study by *McKinsey & Company*, organizations that prioritize adaptability are 23% more likely to outperform competitors during times of disruption.

Consider Mia, a seasoned event planner whose career was upended when the pandemic struck. Overnight, her in-person events were canceled, leaving her business in jeopardy. Instead of dwelling on the losses, Mia displayed remarkable resilience and adaptability by pivoting to virtual events. She invested time in learning new tools, such as video conferencing platforms and virtual engagement strategies, and reimagined how events could deliver value in a digital format. Her ability to adapt not only saved her business but positioned her as a leader in the virtual event space. Mia's story highlights the transformative potential of resilience and adaptability in turning setbacks into opportunities.

Building Resilience and Adaptability

Developing resilience and adaptability requires a proactive mindset and deliberate effort. Start by reframing challenges as opportunities for growth rather than threats to stability. For example, instead of viewing a project delay as a failure, consider it a chance to refine your approach or develop new skills. Building a support system is also crucial; research from *Gallup* shows that employees with strong social connections at work are 20% more resilient to stress and 30% more adaptable to change. Regularly practicing mindfulness and stress-management techniques can further enhance your capacity to remain calm and focused during times of uncertainty.

Thriving in a Dynamic World

Resilience and adaptability are no longer optional—they are critical to thriving in a world that demands constant evolution. By embracing these qualities, you can navigate challenges with confidence, turn disruptions into opportunities, and position yourself as a leader in times of change. Analytics underscore the importance of these traits: professionals who demonstrate high levels of resilience and adaptability are 45% more likely to achieve career advancement and 30% more likely to report personal well-being. This week, we'll explore actionable strategies to cultivate these skills, empowering you to not only survive but thrive in an unpredictable world.

What Is Resilience?

Resilience is the ability to recover from setbacks, adapt to change, and keep moving forward despite difficulties.

Characteristics of Resilient Individuals

1. **Optimism**: Viewing challenges as opportunities for growth.
2. **Emotional Regulation**: Managing stress and maintaining focus under pressure.
3. **Problem-Solving Skills**: Finding solutions in the face of obstacles.

Example: James, a graphic designer, faced rejection when pitching a bold idea to a client. Instead of giving up, he revised his proposal based on the feedback and won the client over with an improved version.

Building Resilience

- Develop a growth mindset: See failures as learning opportunities.
- Strengthen your support system: Lean on colleagues, mentors, or friends during tough times.

Adaptability: The Key to Staying Relevant

Adaptability is the ability to adjust to new conditions or unexpected changes while maintaining productivity and creativity.

Why Adaptability Matters

- **Professional Growth**: The most adaptable employees are often the first to embrace new opportunities.
- **Leadership**: Leaders who adapt inspire confidence and guide their teams effectively through transitions.

Practicing Adaptability

1. **Be Open to Feedback**: Embrace suggestions for improvement and adjust your approach accordingly.
2. **Expand Your Skills**: Stay ahead by learning new tools, technologies, or methodologies.
3. **Stay Calm in Uncertainty**: Focus on what you can control and let go of what you can't.

STORY

Embracing Change to Lead Transformation

When Sarah's company decided to adopt a new enterprise re-source planning (ERP) software, the announcement sent ripples of anxiety through the team. The new platform promised to streamline processes and improve efficiency, but it also required everyone to adapt to unfamiliar technology. Like many of her colleagues, Sarah initially felt overwhelmed. The interface was confusing, the functionality complex, and the learning curve steep. For someone who had become comfortable with the old systems, the change felt daunting.

But Sarah realized that resisting the shift would only hinder her growth and her team's success. Determined to adapt, she dove into learning the software. She started with company-provided training resources, then supplemented her knowledge with online tutorials and forums. Sarah also reached out to the software provider's support team for deeper insights into how the platform could be tailored to meet her company's needs. Her effort wasn't just about mastering the technical skills—it was about understanding how the new system could improve workflows and create value for the organization.

As Sarah became more proficient, her colleagues began turning to her for help. Recognizing this as an opportunity, she proposed organizing training sessions to share what she had learned. With her manager's support, Sarah developed easy-to-follow guides and hosted weekly workshops where team members could ask questions and practice using the platform. She also introduced a "tip of the week" email, sharing quick tricks to help her colleagues navigate the system more effectively.

The results were transformative. Within three months, the team's adoption rate increased by 40%, and operational errors tied to the transition dropped by 25%. The new software, once seen as a hurdle, became a tool that improved collaboration and efficiency. Sarah's leadership during this period didn't go unnoticed. Her proactive approach earned her recognition as a change leader, and she was invited to join the company's cross-functional innovation committee, tasked with driving future technology upgrades.

Sarah's journey underscores a critical lesson: embracing change and taking initiative can turn challenges into opportunities for growth and leadership. By becoming a resource for her team, Sarah not only built her own technical skills but also fostered a culture of collaboration and adaptability. Her ability to see beyond the immediate discomfort of change and focus on its long-term benefits positioned her as a key contributor to her organization's success.

This story also highlights a broader trend: employees who embrace continuous learning and adaptability are more likely to thrive in an ever-changing workplace. Research shows that organizations with high levels of employee engagement during major transitions experience 21% higher productivity. Sarah's example demonstrates how individual initiative can ripple outward, driving positive outcomes for both people and the business as a whole.

Strategies to Build Resilience and Adaptability

1. Cultivate a Positive Mindset
- Practice gratitude to shift your focus from problems to solutions.
- Reframe setbacks: Instead of "I failed," think "I learned what doesn't work."

2. Develop Flexibility in Problem-Solving
- Explore multiple solutions to challenges.
- Use brainstorming techniques to generate creative ideas.

Example: A startup team faced delays in product manufacturing. By brainstorming alternative supply chain options, they minimized the impact and met their launch deadline.

3. Strengthen Emotional Intelligence
- Recognize and regulate your emotions during stressful situations.
- Empathize with others to navigate team dynamics during change.

4. Focus on Self-Care
- Resilience is tied to physical and mental well-being. Ensure you're getting adequate rest, exercise, and relaxation.

Overcoming Resistance to Change

Change can be unsettling, but it's also inevitable. Learning to embrace change makes you more adaptable and resilient.

Addressing Fear of the Unknown

- Focus on the opportunities that change presents, such as learning new skills or gaining fresh perspectives.
- Break down big changes into manageable steps to reduce overwhelm.

Learning to Let Go

- Accept that not every plan will succeed and be willing to pivot.
- Recognize when to stop investing energy in a losing strategy.

STORY

Alex, a project manager, was tasked with leading a failing initiative. After careful evaluation, he recommended reallocating resources to a more viable project. This decision, though difficult, saved the company significant time and money.

Story Example: Rising Through Adversity

Elena, a mid-level HR professional, faced a major challenge when her company announced layoffs. As one of the employees retained, she was tasked with rebuilding morale in the aftermath.

Initially, Elena felt overwhelmed by the responsibility. Instead of succumbing to stress, she sought guidance from mentors, focused on small wins, and prioritized transparent communication with her team. She also introduced wellness initiatives to support employees during the transition.

Through her resilience and adaptability, Elena not only helped stabilize the team but also gained recognition from leadership for her efforts, eventually earning a promotion to senior HR manager.

Turning Challenges into Opportunities

Resilience and adaptability are not fixed traits—they are skills you can develop and refine. By cultivating a positive mindset, embracing flexibility, and focusing on self-care, you'll be better equipped to navigate challenges and thrive in change.

This week, challenge yourself to:

1. Identify a recent setback and reflect on what you learned from it.
2. Embrace a small change in your work routine to practice adaptability.

Remember, resilience is about bouncing back, and adaptability is about moving forward. Together, they are the tools that will help you thrive in any environment.

WEEK 8 CHALLENGE

Resilience and Adaptability

Visual Guide: Resilience Growth Cycle

Phase	Example Action
Reflect	Identify lessons from a recent challenge.
Adapt	Change one routine or process to improve outcomes.
Reframe	See setbacks as opportunities for growth.

Checklist:

- Write down 3 lessons from a recent challenge.
- Make one small adjustment in your work process.
- Start a gratitude journal with 3 entries daily.

MINDFUL MOTION:
THE ART OF LIVING WELL

Techniques for Mental Wellbeing
Related to Yoga and Tai Chi

Affirmation:
"I embrace the harmony of movement and breath, cultivating peace within and resilience for life's challenges."

Motivational Quote
"True wellbeing is the art of balancing the mind, body, and spirit. In stillness and flow, we discover our inner strength."

In today's fast-paced world, the quest for mental wellbeing is more important than ever. Ancient practices such as Yoga and Tai Chi offer time-tested pathways to achieve a harmonious balance between the mind, body, and spirit. These practices not only enhance physical health but also promote mental clarity, emotional resilience, and inner peace. By focusing on mindful movement, breath control, and meditation, both Yoga and Tai Chi provide holistic approaches to managing stress and fostering mental wellbeing.

Yoga, with its origins in India, integrates physical postures (asanas), breath control techniques (pranayama), and meditation to cultivate a state of mindfulness and self-awareness. It is a practice that encourages individuals to connect deeply with their inner selves while also building strength, flexibility, and balance. Whether through a vigorous flow or a restorative sequence, Yoga empowers practitioners to release tension, quiet the mind, and foster a sense of calm in their daily lives.

Similarly, Tai Chi, rooted in the ancient martial arts traditions of China, emphasizes slow, deliberate movements synchronized with deep, intentional breathing. This gentle yet profound practice is often described as "meditation in motion," as it encourages practitioners to stay present in the moment while enhancing physical coordination, balance, and mental focus. Together, Yoga and Tai Chi offer complementary tools for nurturing mental wellbeing, enabling individuals to navigate life's challenges with grace, strength, and mindfulness.

Benefits for Mental Wellbeing

1. **Stress Reduction**: Both practices activate the parasympathetic nervous system, reducing cortisol levels and calming the mind.
2. **Improved Focus and Clarity**: Mindful movements and breath control enhance concentration and reduce mental clutter.
3. **Emotional Balance**: Regular practice encourages self-awareness and emotional regulation, leading to improved resilience.
4. **Enhanced Sleep Quality**: Relaxation techniques from both practices can reduce insomnia and promote restorative sleep.

Techniques for Incorporating Yoga and Tai Chi for Mental Wellbeing

Yoga Techniques

1. **Pranayama (Breath Control)**
   - **Technique**: Try "Alternate Nostril Breathing" (Nadi Shodhana) by closing one nostril, inhaling through the other, and alternating.
   - **Benefits**: Balances energy, reduces anxiety, and enhances focus.

2. **Asanas (Postures)**
   - **Child's Pose (Balasana)**: Promotes relaxation and reduces stress.
   - **Tree Pose (Vrksasana)**: Enhances balance and focus.

3. **Meditation**
   - **Technique**: Practice mindfulness meditation by sitting comfortably, focusing on your breath, and gently returning your attention to it when distracted.
   - **Benefits**: Reduces mental chatter, improves emotional stability.

Tai Chi Techniques

1. **Flowing Movements**
   - **Technique**: Perform "Wave Hands Like Clouds" with smooth, rhythmic hand motions, shifting weight gently between legs.

- o **Benefits**: Encourages relaxation, improves coordination, and calms the mind.

2. **Breathing Integration**
   - o **Technique**: Practice deep, diaphragmatic breathing in sync with movements, inhaling through the nose and exhaling slowly through the mouth.
   - o **Benefits**: Reduces stress and oxygenates the brain.

3. **Standing Meditation (Zhan Zhuang)**
   - o **Technique**: Stand still in a natural posture, focusing on aligning the spine and feeling rooted to the ground.
   - o **Benefits**: Builds mental resilience and physical stability.

Steps to Start and Maintain a Practice for Mental Wellbeing

Step 1: Create a Quiet Space
- Designate a peaceful area in your home for practice. Keep it uncluttered and soothing with natural elements like plants or soft lighting.

Step 2: Start with Short Sessions
- Begin with 10-15 minutes daily. Gradually increase the duration as your comfort level grows.

Step 3: Follow Guided Resources
- Use beginner-friendly videos or apps for Yoga and Tai Chi to ensure proper form and technique.

Step 4: Focus on Breathing
- Always coordinate breath with movement. If in doubt, prioritize slow and deep breathing.

Step 5: Incorporate Mindfulness
- Stay present during each movement or posture. Let go of distractions and focus on how your body feels.

Step 6: Join a community / group
- Consider attending local Yoga or Tai Chi classes for guidance and motivation. Online communities can also provide support.

Step 7: Reflect on Your Progress
- Keep a journal to note mental and emotional changes. Reflecting helps reinforce the benefits and motivates continued practice.

Step 8: Combine Practices
- Blend yoga postures and Tai Chi movements into your routine, creating a holistic approach to mental wellbeing.

Yoga and Tai Chi are transformative practices that offer powerful tools for enhancing mental wellbeing. By adopting these techniques and following the outlined steps, you can achieve greater peace, focus, and emotional balance in daily life.

WEEK 9

CRAFTING YOUR
PERSONAL BRAND

CRAFTING YOUR PERSONAL BRAND

In today's interconnected and highly competitive world, your personal brand is your calling card. It represents who you are, what you stand for, and the unique value you bring to the table. A well-crafted personal brand isn't just about self-promotion—it's about authentically sharing your expertise, values, and vision. Whether you're climbing the corporate ladder, launching a business, or striving to make an impact in your industry, a strong personal brand can help you stand out, build trust, and open doors to transformative opportunities.

What is Personal Branding?

Personal branding is the intentional effort to shape how others perceive you. It encompasses your professional reputation, your online presence, and even the way you communicate. According to a study by *CareerBuilder*, 70% of employers use social media to screen candidates during the hiring process, and 50% of them choose not to hire someone based on their online presence. This underscores the importance of curating a brand that aligns with your goals and values. A strong personal brand isn't just a tool for career advancement—it's a way to create connections, showcase your expertise, and amplify your impact.

Consider Sophia, a financial analyst with aspirations of becoming a thought leader in sustainability finance. By defining her personal brand, she carved a niche for herself in a highly specialized field. Sophia began by writing LinkedIn posts on green investing, offering actionable insights that demonstrated her knowledge and passion. She joined industry panels to share her expertise and expanded her network by engaging with like-minded professionals. Her efforts not only positioned her as a trusted voice in sustainability finance but also caught the attention of her firm's leadership. As a result, Sophia was invited to lead a high-profile sustainability project, aligning her personal brand with her professional aspirations.

Building and Communicating Your Brand

Crafting a personal brand begins with self-reflection. Ask yourself: What are my strengths? What values do I want to communicate? What problems can I solve for others? Defining your brand also involves identifying your target audience— whether it's potential employers, industry peers, or clients— and tailoring your message to resonate with them. Analytics from *LinkedIn* reveal that professionals who post consistently and authentically see a 56% increase in profile views and are 31% more likely to be contacted for opportunities. This demonstrates the power of visibility and authenticity in building a compelling brand.

To communicate your brand effectively, leverage platforms that align with your goals. Social media, industry events, blogs, and podcasts are powerful tools for sharing your expertise and expanding your reach. For instance, regularly posting content that highlights your insights or achievements can position you as a thought leader in your field. Networking strategically—both online and offline—further reinforces your brand by associating it with influential peers and mentors.

Elevating Your Brand

Maintaining and elevating your personal brand is an ongoing process. Continually refine your messaging to align with evolving goals and industry trends. Seek feedback from trusted colleagues and mentors to ensure that your brand resonates with your target audience. Analytics from *Forbes* show that 85% of executives with strong personal brands attribute their success to consistent messaging and regular engagement with their audience. By staying visible, relevant, and authentic, you ensure that your personal brand evolves alongside your career.

Your Brand, Your Legacy

Ultimately, your personal brand is the story you tell the world about your values, expertise, and aspirations. It's not just about what you do—it's about the impact you leave behind. By investing in your personal brand, you create opportunities, foster connections, and position yourself as a leader in your field. This week, we'll dive into actionable strategies to define, communicate, and elevate your personal brand, helping you align your professional goals with a compelling and authentic narrative.

Defining Your Personal Brand

Before you can build a personal brand, you need clarity about your unique value.

1. Self-Reflection

Ask yourself:

- What are my core strengths?
- What values guide my work and life?
- How do I want to be perceived by colleagues, clients, and peers?

Example: Raj, a software developer, wanted to stand out in the competitive tech space. After reflecting, he realized his strength was simplifying complex concepts. He branded himself as a communicator who bridges the gap between tech and business, gaining recognition as a presenter at conferences.

2. Identifying Your Niche

Your personal brand should focus on an area where you excel. A niche doesn't limit you—it amplifies your expertise.

- What are you passionate about?
- Where do your skills create the most impact?

3. Crafting Your Elevator Pitch

Summarize your brand in a clear, concise way.

- Format: "I help [target audience] achieve [results] by [unique approach]."
- Example: "I help startups scale sustainably by streamlining their financial processes and optimizing growth strategies."

Communicating Your Brand Effectively

Once you've defined your brand, it's time to share it consistently and authentically.

1. Leveraging Social Media

- Use platforms like LinkedIn to showcase your expertise.
- Share original insights, industry updates, or thought-provoking questions.
- Engage with others' posts by commenting or sharing.

STORY

How Consistent Personal Branding Elevated Maria's Career

Maria, a talented data scientist with a passion for artificial intelligence, had always been fascinated by its potential to revolutionize healthcare. While her work focused on algorithm development and predictive analytics for patient outcomes, Maria wanted to establish herself as a thought leader in the field. Recognizing the power of social media and professional networks, she decided to share her insights regularly on platforms like LinkedIn. Over six months, Maria consistently posted about AI applications in healthcare, covering topics such as predictive diagnostics, personalized treatment plans, and ethical considerations in medical AI.

Her posts gained traction, earning her an engaged audience of industry professionals, academics, and innovators. On average, Maria's articles and insights reached over 10,000 views per month, with many generating robust discussions in the comments. By incorporating recent research, industry trends, and real-world examples, she positioned herself as a knowledgeable and forward-thinking expert. Additionally, she actively engaged with her network by commenting on and sharing posts from other professionals, further amplifying her visibility. According to LinkedIn analytics, Maria's profile views increased by 65%, and her connections grew by 40%, signaling her growing influence in the healthcare AI community.

One day, Maria's consistent efforts paid off in a big way. A recruiter from a leading biotech company reached out to her, referencing one of her posts about leveraging AI to optimize clinical trials. The recruiter was impressed by her expertise and her ability to communicate complex ideas effectively. After a series of interviews, Maria was offered a senior role focused on developing AI-driven solutions for healthcare innovation—a position that aligned perfectly with her skills and passions. Maria's story

illustrates the power of personal branding and consistent content sharing in creating career opportunities. Studies show that 70% of employers use social media to research candidates, and professionals with strong online presences are 27% more likely to be approached for job opportunities. By leveraging her knowledge and building her personal brand, Maria not only advanced her career but also became a recognized voice in her field.

2. Networking and Public Engagement

- Attend industry events and introduce yourself with confidence.
- Volunteer to speak at panels, webinars, or company workshops.

3. Consistency Across Platforms

- Align your LinkedIn profile, resume, and any public bios with your brand message.

- Use a professional headshot and a headline that highlights your expertise.

Quick Tip: Review your online presence to ensure it reflects your brand. Google your name—what do the search results say about you?

Elevating Your Personal Brand

A strong personal brand isn't static—it evolves as you grow.

1. Showcasing Accomplishments

- Highlight measurable results: "Increased sales by 20% in six months through targeted campaigns."
- Share testimonials or endorsements from clients or colleagues.

2. Building Thought Leadership

- Write articles, blogs, or whitepapers on your area of expertise.
- Host or guest on podcasts to share your insights.

Example: Ethan, a supply chain expert, wrote a LinkedIn article on post-pandemic logistics trends. The post went viral, leading to invitations for guest lectures and consulting gigs.

3. Maintaining Authenticity

Stay true to your values and voice. Audiences resonate with authenticity. Avoid over-polishing your brand to the point where it feels impersonal.

Overcoming Branding Challenges

Building a personal brand can feel daunting, but addressing common challenges can make the process smoother.

1. Impostor Syndrome

- Remind yourself that expertise is a journey, not a destination.
- Focus on what you know and the unique perspective you bring.

2. Fear of Self-Promotion

- Shift your mindset: You're sharing value, not bragging.
- Start small by sharing achievements in a team meeting or posting a quick LinkedIn update.

3. Lack of Time

- Dedicate 30 minutes a week to brand-building activities, such as updating your LinkedIn or attending a networking event.

STORY

A Personal Branding Success

David, a skilled IT consultant, had spent over a decade honing his technical expertise, yet he often felt invisible in a competitive field. Despite his extensive experience, he struggled to land leadership roles or gain recognition beyond his immediate network. Frustrated and unsure how to advance his career, David attended a personal branding workshop that shifted his perspective. The workshop emphasized the importance of identifying a niche and consistently communicating value to a target audience. Inspired, David decided to focus on a growing area of need: cybersecurity for small businesses, a niche often overlooked by larger consulting firms.

Determined to establish himself as an expert, David began sharing actionable insights on LinkedIn. His posts, like "5 Simple Steps to Protect Your Business from Cyber Threats" and "Affordable Tools for Small-Business Cybersecurity," resonated with small-business owners and IT professionals alike. Recognizing the value of direct engagement, he also hosted free webinars, where he shared case studies and answered questions from local entrepreneurs. Over six months, his efforts gained momentum: his LinkedIn posts averaged 8,000 views, his webinars attracted dozens of participants, and he received multiple invitations to speak at local business events. David's visibility and credibility in his niche grew exponentially.

The breakthrough came when a recruiter from a prominent tech company reached out to him. The company had been searching for someone to lead their newly formed small-business security division, and David's online presence made him an obvious candidate. During the interview process, his ability to articulate complex cybersecurity concepts in a relatable way and his passion for empowering small businesses set him apart. David was offered the role, which not only aligned with his expertise but also

provided him with the leadership platform he had been seeking. His story demonstrates how a well-defined and consistently communicated personal brand can elevate a career, opening doors that might otherwise remain closed. Research shows that professionals who focus on personal branding are 31% more likely to attract career opportunities, and David's journey is a testament to the transformative power of intentional self-promotion.

Own Your Narrative

Your personal brand is your story—one that you control. By reflecting on your strengths, communicating your message effectively, and staying consistent, you can position yourself as a trusted expert and leader.

This week, challenge yourself to:

1. Write a draft of your personal elevator pitch.
2. Post one thought-provoking update on LinkedIn or another professional platform.

Remember, your brand is a reflection of your unique value. Share it with confidence, and the right opportunities will follow.

WEEK 9 CHALLENGE
Crafting Your Personal Brand

Visual Guide: Personal Branding Checklist

Area	Your Progress
Statement	Write a one-sentence branding statement.
Digital Presence	Update your LinkedIn and social media profiles.
Engagement	Post one professional insight or resource.

Checklist:

- Write your personal brand statement.
- Update your LinkedIn profile headline and summary.
- Engage with at least 3 posts from your network.

MINDFUL MOTION:
THE ART OF LIVING WELL

Weight Management– Approaches to maintaining a healthy weight.

Affirmation:
I love the skin I'm in.

Motivational Quote:
"The only successful way to reach and maintain a healthy weight is to find what works for you." FinetoFit.com

Achieving and maintaining a healthy weight is essential for overall health and wellness. It can enhance your quality of life and lower your risk of various health issues. However, maintaining a healthy weight can often be challenging, requiring a long-term commitment to healthy habits.

Trying to Lose Weight

There is no one-size-fits-all approach to weight loss, as different methods work for different people. The key is to consume fewer calories than your body requires to function, which creates a calorie deficit and promotes weight loss. Calories (kcal) are the energy obtained from food and drink, and this energy fuels the body's activities.

Research shows that the most successful weight loss strategies are those that can be sustained over time. Therefore, it's important to find a weight loss plan that fits your lifestyle and is enjoyable for you.

When trying to lose weight, the average person should aim to reduce their daily calorie intake by about 500- 600 kcal per day.

That means reducing calories from the recommended daily allowance to:

- 1600-1800 kcal/day for men
- 1200-1500 kcal/day for women

Avoid Fad Diets

Fad diets promise quick weight loss but often lack scientific evidence and can be nutritionally unbalanced. These diets are typically difficult to stick with in the long term and can lead to nutritional deficiencies. Instead of following a fad diet, focus on a sustainable, balanced approach to eating.

Tips for Healthy Weight Loss

- Initial goal should be to lose 10% of baseline weight. i.e., if current weight is 180 lbs, goal is to lose 18 lbs. Safe weight loss is 1-2 lbs per week.
- Set Realistic, Gradual Goals: Start with small, achievable goals to help you lose weight safely and increase your chances of long-term success.
- Eat Regular, Balanced Meals: Aim for three balanced meals each day to maintain stable energy levels and avoid overeating.

- Time Your Meals: Try to have meals at regular intervals, 4-5 hours apart and only snack when you're physically hungry, 2 hours between meals.

Healthy Food Substitutes

When working to lose weight, replacing high-calorie foods with healthier options can help.

Consider swapping:

- Chips and dips for crunchy vegetables like peppers, celery, cucumbers, sugar snap peas, and carrots with low-fat hummus.
- A chocolate bar for a handful of unsalted nuts
- High-calorie drinks like lattes or mochas for a lower-calorie Americano

Portion Control

Learning to manage portion sizes is a crucial part of successful weight loss. While portion needs vary depending on factors like age and activity level, here are some general guidelines for portion sizes:

- Lean Protein: Palm size portion (chicken/turkey white meat/no skin; beef or pork loin, fish.
- Non-starchy vegetables: ½ plate (dark leafy greens, broccoli, carrots, tomatoes, green beans, cabbage, zucchini, eggplant.
- Starch: ¼ plate (rice, pasta, potatoes, corn, peas, butter nut squash). No more than 1 cup total.

- Fruit: ¼ plate or less.

Using smaller plates, 9 inches in diameter, can also reduce portion sizes and, in turn, reduce calorie intake.

Minimize Distractions While Eating

Eating while watching TV or using other technology can lead to overeating. Mindless eating, where we don't focus on our food, often results in consuming more calories. Consuming 100 extra calories daily can lead to 10 pounds weight gain in one year.

Plan Your Meals

Planning meals ahead of time ensures you have the right foods available when needed. Consider the following strategies:

- Use a weekly meal planner
- Make a shopping list to stay organized
- Prepare and freeze meals for later
- Try cooking with an air fryer or slow cooker

Avoid shopping while hungry, as this can lead to impulse buys, especially unhealthy foods high in fat, sugar, or salt.

Stay Active

Physical activity offers numerous health benefits and can be a valuable part of a weight loss or maintenance plan. It is recommended that adults aim for at least 150 minutes of moderate-intensity aerobic activity each week, which can include walking, cycling, or even activities like heavy housework. Alternatively,

75 minutes of vigorous exercise, such as running or a game of football, can be equally effective.

Strength and balance exercises, such as weightlifting or yoga, should be included two-three time a week to maintain muscle, bone, and joint health, reducing the risk of frailty and falls as we age.

Remember, "Something is Better than Nothing." Find activities you enjoy and start with small steps — it's never too late to begin.

WEEK 10

LIFELONG LEARNING
& SKILL BUILDING

WEEK 10

LIFELONG LEARNING AND SKILL BUILDING

The Value of Continuous Growth

The world is constantly evolving, and so are the skills needed to thrive in it. Lifelong learning isn't just a strategy for career advancement—it's a mindset that keeps you adaptable, relevant, and inspired.

Take Amanda, a marketing professional who noticed a growing demand for data-driven campaigns. Despite having no background in analytics, she committed to learning data visualization tools. Over time, her new skills not only enhanced her value at work but also opened doors to roles she never thought possible.

This week, we'll explore the importance of lifelong learning and practical ways to continuously build your skill set.

Why Lifelong Learning Matters

1. Staying Relevant in a Changing World

Industries evolve rapidly. Learning new skills ensures you remain competitive, no matter how the landscape shifts.

Example: When cloud computing became mainstream, IT professionals who learned cloud architecture gained a significant edge over those who stuck to legacy systems.

2. Unlocking New Opportunities

Continuous learning expands your career options. Whether it's a certification, a new language, or a technical skill, each addition to your toolkit makes you more versatile.

3. Boosting Creativity and Confidence

Learning fosters curiosity and problem-solving. It also enhances confidence by proving that you can master new challenges.

Quick Insight: Research shows that engaging in lifelong learning reduces stress and improves mental health by creating a sense of purpose.

Identifying Your Learning Goals

To learn effectively, it's important to target skills that align with your career aspirations and personal interests.

1. Assessing Skill Gaps

- Ask yourself: What skills are essential in my field today? What skills will be critical in the next 5–10 years?
- Use feedback from colleagues or mentors to identify areas for improvement.

2. Setting SMART Learning Goals

- **Specific**: "Learn Python for data analysis."
- **Measurable**: "Complete an online Python course within three months."
- **Achievable**: Start with beginner-level resources if you're new to coding.
- **Relevant**: Ensure the skill aligns with your role or aspirations.
- **Time-Bound**: Dedicate 5 hours weekly to the course.

Effective Learning Strategies

1. Leverage Online Resources

- Platforms like Coursera, LinkedIn Learning, and Udemy offer courses across disciplines.
- For tech skills, sites like Codecademy or Khan Academy are invaluable.

2. Learn Through Experience

- Take on stretch assignments at work to develop new competencies.
- Volunteer for cross-functional projects to broaden your perspective.

Example: Jason, an HR specialist, joined a task force to design a new company intranet. The experience helped him learn project management skills he later used to lead his own initiatives.

3. Embrace Microlearning

- Break learning into manageable chunks: Watch a 10-minute tutorial, read an article, or complete a single module.
- Apps like Duolingo or Blinkist make it easy to learn on the go.

Building a Learning Ecosystem

To sustain lifelong learning, create an environment that encourages growth.

1. Find Mentors and Coaches

- Seek guidance from professionals who've mastered skills you're pursuing.
- Mentors can provide personalized advice, while coaches offer structured support.

2. Join Communities of Practice

- Participate in industry groups, forums, or networking events to learn from peers.
- Platforms like Meetup or Reddit have active communities for almost every niche.

3. Develop a Feedback Loop

- Regularly review your progress and adjust your approach.
- Share your learning journey with peers or mentors for additional accountability.

Overcoming Barriers to Learning

1. Lack of Time

- Prioritize learning by blocking time on your calendar.
- Use "dead time" (e.g., commutes) to listen to podcasts or audiobooks.

2. Fear of Starting

- Break large goals into smaller steps to reduce overwhelm.
- Remember, every expert was once a beginner.

3. Financial Constraints

- Many high-quality resources, like YouTube tutorials or free online courses, cost nothing.
- Employers often sponsor professional development—don't hesitate to ask.

Example: After losing his job, Marco used free resources to learn graphic design. Within a year, he launched a successful freelance career.

STORY

The Power of Learning

Diane, an experienced operations manager, had built a strong reputation for ensuring efficiency and precision in her company's logistics processes. However, when her organization announced a transition to a new logistics management system, she found herself in unfamiliar territory. The platform was complex, and Diane had no prior experience with it. The initial training sessions felt overwhelming, leaving her unsure of how to lead her team through the change. For the first time in years, Diane felt out of her depth.

Determined to overcome this challenge, Diane took a proactive approach. She enrolled in a free, in-depth training course offered by the software provider, dedicating evenings and weekends to mastering the system. Realizing the value of peer learning, she also joined an online user group where professionals from various industries shared insights, troubleshooting tips, and best practices. Through consistent engagement in these forums, Diane not only gained technical expertise but also discovered innovative ways to tailor the platform to her company's needs. For example, she implemented a custom reporting feature that reduced manual data entry by 40% and saved her team hours of work each week.

Within a few months, Diane's efforts paid off. She became her team's go-to resource for navigating the new system, providing guidance and solutions that minimized disruptions during the transition. Her proactive learning and leadership skills didn't go unnoticed. Diane's manager commended her adaptability and initiative, assigning her to lead future system implementations across the company's regional offices. This new leadership role not only expanded her influence within the organization but also positioned her as a model of continuous learning and innovation.

Diane's story illustrates the transformative power of embracing challenges as opportunities for growth. Research shows that employees who engage in self-directed learning are 21% more likely to be promoted and 15% more likely to take on leadership roles. By seeking knowledge, leveraging available resources, and sharing her expertise, Diane turned a potentially overwhelming situation into a steppingstone for career advancement. Her experience highlights a crucial lesson for professionals: the willingness to learn and adapt is a cornerstone of success in an ever-changing workplace.

Learning Is a Journey

Lifelong learning is not just about acquiring new skills—it's about cultivating a mindset of curiosity, adaptability, and growth that fuels both personal and professional success. In a rapidly changing world, the ability to learn continuously has become more essential than ever. According to a LinkedIn Workplace Learning Report, 94% of employees say they would stay longer at a company that invests in their learning and development, highlighting the value of embracing learning as an ongoing journey.

Whether it's mastering a technical skill, enhancing emotional intelligence, or exploring a new hobby, lifelong learning enriches our lives by keeping us engaged and prepared for whatever comes next.

This week, take a step toward fostering your own learning journey by setting a small, actionable goal.

Start by identifying one skill you'd like to develop—perhaps improving your presentation skills, learning a new programming language, or exploring creative writing. Then, commit to taking the first step: enroll in a course on platforms like Coursera or Udemy, watch a free tutorial on YouTube, or seek guidance from a colleague or mentor who excels in that area. Research shows that even dedicating as little as 30 minutes a day to focused learning can lead to significant improvements over time, making this a manageable commitment for even the busiest schedules.

The beauty of lifelong learning lies in its dual benefits: it prepares you for future challenges while enriching your present. The process of discovering new ideas and expanding your capabilities brings a sense of accomplishment and confidence. It also enhances problem-solving skills, creativity, and resilience—qualities that are invaluable in both personal and professional contexts. As the ancient philosopher Plutarch once said, "The mind is not a vessel to be filled, but a fire to be kindled." Embrace the journey of learning, and let it ignite your potential, one step at a time.

WEEK 10 CHALLENGE

Lifelong Learning and Skill Building

Visual Guide: Skill Development Plan

Step	Action
Identify Skill	What do you want to learn or improve?
Set Goal	Define a SMART learning goal.
Choose Resources	Select courses, books, or mentors for guidance.

Checklist:

- Choose one skill to learn.
- Spend 30 minutes exploring learning resources.
- Apply the skill to a real-world task or project.

MINDFUL MOTION:
THE ART OF LIVING WELL

Gluten Free, Don't Believe the Hype

Affirmation
I am always learning.

Motivational Quote
"To eat is a necessity, but to eat intelligently is an art." – Francois La Rochefoucauld

What you need to know: Gluten = a protein found in wheat, barley and rye.

- Gluten is not harmful unless you have: Celiac disease or gluten intolerance.

> Celiac Disease is a chronic condition that causes the body to have an autoimmune reaction to gluten, which may result in damage to the small intestine, preventing the absorption of nutrients from food.

> Gluten intolerance is when you feel sick after eating gluten. Symptoms include bloating, stomach pain, nausea/vomiting, diarrhea/constipation, headache. About 6% of the U.S. population is gluten intolerant.

- Gluten itself does not make you gain weight.

- Gluten-free products still contain loads of sugar and fat.

So, skip the gluten-free products and eat a well-balanced diet full of fruits, vegetables, and 100% whole grains! Look for products that contain more than 3 grams of fiber per serving.

Some varieties of whole grains include quinoa, brown rice, wild rice, oatmeal, whole grain breakfast cereals, whole wheat bread, pasta, or crackers.

*Weight loss is achieved when expend more calories than you take in.

WEEK 11

LEADING WITH
INTEGRITY &
PURPOSE

LEADING WITH INTEGRITY AND PURPOSE

Leadership Rooted in Values

Leadership is more than a title—it's the ability to inspire and guide others toward a shared vision. But what separates great leaders from the rest? Integrity and purpose.

Consider Alisha, a regional sales manager who faced an ethical dilemma when a senior colleague proposed inflating quarterly numbers. Instead of compromising her principles, Alisha spoke up, risking backlash. Her decision not only protected the company's reputation but also earned her the trust and respect of her team.

This week, we'll explore how to lead authentically, foster trust, and create a lasting impact by grounding leadership in integrity and purpose.

What Does It Mean to Lead with Integrity?

Integrity is the cornerstone of ethical leadership. It means acting with honesty, fairness, and consistency, even when it's inconvenient.

Core Characteristics of Integrity in Leadership

1. **Honesty**: Being transparent about challenges, decisions, and mistakes.
2. **Accountability**: Owning up to your actions and their consequences.
3. **Fairness**: Treating everyone with respect and impartiality.

Example: During a project delay, a leader who admits responsibility and outlines a recovery plan demonstrates integrity, earning the team's trust and cooperation.

The Power of Purpose in Leadership

Purpose gives direction to your actions and inspires others to follow. A leader with purpose knows why they do what they do and connects that "why" to the team's goals.

Benefits of Purpose-Driven Leadership

- **Increased Engagement**: Teams are more motivated when they understand the mission.
- **Stronger Decision-Making**: Purpose acts as a compass, guiding choices during uncertainty.

Finding Your Leadership Purpose

- Reflect on your values: What principles guide your actions?

- Identify your impact: What difference do you want to make through your leadership?

Example: Marcus, a nonprofit director, defined his purpose as "empowering underprivileged communities through education." This clarity helped him align his team's efforts and attract like-minded supporters.

Practical Ways to Lead with Integrity and Purpose

1. Communicate Honestly and Transparently

- Share successes and setbacks openly with your team.
- Avoid sugarcoating problems; instead, focus on solutions.

2. Model Ethical Behavior

- Lead by example. Show integrity through your actions, not just words.
- Address unethical behavior immediately, even when it's uncomfortable.

STORY

Championing Fairness to Build Trust

Sara, a seasoned team leader in a mid-sized tech company, noticed a troubling pattern during performance review cycles. While some employees received glowing feedback and promotions, others felt overlooked despite their hard work. After a closer look, Sara realized that favoritism—whether intentional or subconscious—was influencing the evaluation process. This imbalance was not only unfair but also damaging team morale and creating an atmosphere of distrust.

Determined to address the issue, Sara took the initiative to propose a standardized performance evaluation system. She started by researching best practices in performance management, drawing insights from industry reports and academic studies. According to a Harvard Business Review study, companies that adopt structured performance reviews see a 30% increase in employee satisfaction and a 20% improvement in team productivity. Sara used these findings to build a case for change and secured buy-in from leadership to pilot the new system.

The new process focused on measurable goals, competency-based assessments, and consistent feedback criteria. Sara introduced tools like self-assessment forms, peer reviews, and a scoring rubric to ensure transparency and reduce bias. To roll out the changes effectively, she conducted training sessions with managers and employees, emphasizing the importance of fairness and objectivity. Over time, the impact became evident. Employees reported feeling more valued and understood, and overall trust in the review process increased. Morale improved by 25% according to an internal survey, and turnover rates within the department dropped significantly.

Sara's initiative didn't just enhance performance evaluations—it transformed the team's culture. Her commitment to fairness created a sense of equity and respect that empowered employees to contribute their best work. By addressing favoritism head-on and championing a more inclusive system, Sara proved that leadership isn't just about achieving results; it's about building trust and fostering an environment where everyone feels they have a fair shot at success.

3. Align Actions with Values

- Ensure that your decisions reflect your principles. For instance, if collaboration is a core value, involve your team in decision-making.
- Regularly evaluate whether your leadership style aligns with your purpose.

Fostering Trust Through Integrity

Trust is the foundation of strong teams and organizations. Without trust, even the most talented teams falter.

How to Build Trust as a Leader

1. **Be Consistent**: Follow through on promises and maintain reliability.
2. **Listen Actively**: Show your team that their concerns and ideas matter.
3. **Recognize Effort**: Celebrate achievements and acknowledge contributions.

Example: After consistently recognizing her team's hard work, a manager noticed increased employee satisfaction and decreased turnover rates.

Leading Through Ethical Challenges

Every leader faces moments where integrity is tested. How you respond in these situations defines your character.

Strategies for Navigating Ethical Dilemmas

- **Clarify the Stakes**: What's at risk if you compromise your values?
- **Seek Advice**: Consult mentors or peers to gain perspective.
- **Stand Firm**: Prioritize long-term trust and reputation over short-term gains.

STORY

Values-Driven Leadership in Action

Daniel, a seasoned product manager, and Rachel, a newly promoted operations director, faced pivotal challenges that tested their integrity, leadership, and commitment to long-term success. Both demonstrated the power of value-based decision-making in navigating high-pressure situations while safeguarding both organizational credibility and employee trust.

Daniel's turning point came when he was managing the launch of a highly anticipated product. During the final testing phase, his team discovered critical flaws that could compromise the user experience. Despite mounting pressure from leadership to meet the tight release deadline, Daniel refused to greenlight the product in its flawed state. He knew that rushing a subpar launch could damage the company's reputation and erode customer trust. Instead, Daniel advocated for an extended timeline to address the issues, presenting data on the long-term cost of lost client loyalty versus the short-term expense of delaying the release. Research shows that 59% of customers will stop doing business with a company after multiple poor experiences. By prioritizing quality, Daniel not only protected the company's credibility but also earned the loyalty of clients who valued its commitment to excellence. The product launch, though delayed, was a success, garnering positive reviews and driving a 20% increase in customer retention over the following year.

Rachel's challenge, while different, was no less significant. Newly promoted to operations director, she was tasked with implementing cost-saving measures amidst tightening budgets. Initially, she considered slashing team perks like wellness programs and professional development stipends to meet targets. However, Rachel felt uneasy about this approach, recognizing that such cuts could negatively impact employee morale and engagement. According to a Gallup study, organizations with engaged employees are 21% more profitable. After reflecting on her leadership purpose—to foster a supportive and thriving workplace—Rachel decided to explore alternatives.

Collaborating with her team, Rachel identified inefficiencies in supply chain management and vendor contracts, implementing solutions that reduced costs without sacrificing employee benefits. She also communicated transparently with her team throughout the process, explaining the challenges and inviting their input. This approach not only maintained morale but also strengthened trust and cohesion within the team. By aligning her decisions with her values, Rachel reinforced her credibility as a leader who prioritized both the company's financial health and the well-being of her employees.

Together, Daniel and Rachel's stories illustrate the impact of principled leadership in overcoming difficult decisions. Daniel's insistence on quality safeguarded the company's reputation and strengthened client loyalty, while Rachel's empathetic approach balanced cost-saving with employee satisfaction, driving long-term success. Both leaders demonstrated that when faced with pressure, staying true to one's values is not only the ethical choice but also the strategic one, fostering trust, loyalty, and sustainable results.

Lead with Your North Star

Leadership with integrity and purpose isn't just about making the right choices—it's about inspiring others to do the same. By staying true to your values and fostering trust, you can create a positive impact that lasts far beyond your tenure.

This week, challenge yourself to:

1. Reflect on your leadership purpose. Write it down in one sentence.
2. Identify one way you can align your actions more closely with your values.

Remember, great leadership is a journey. By leading with integrity and purpose, you'll not only achieve results but also leave a legacy of trust and inspiration.

WEEK 11 CHALLENGE
Leading with Integrity and Purpose

Visual Guide: Purpose Alignment Map

Area	Action
Values	Define your top 3 leadership values.
Decisions	Align one decision this week with those values.
Impact	Identify how your actions affect others positively.

Checklist:

- Write your leadership purpose in one sentence.
- Take one action that aligns with your core values.
- Reflect on how your purpose-driven actions influence others.

MINDFUL MOTION:
THE ART OF LIVING WELL

Plant-Based and Vegan Diets -
Exploring benefits and best practices of plant-focused nutrition.

Affirmation:
Today I will take steps to improve my health.

Motivational Quote:
"To eat is a necessity, but to eat intelligently is an art." – Francois La Rochefoucauld

Vegetarian diets encompass a variety of plant-derived foods and exclude some or all foods derived from animals. More specifically, vegetarian diets exclude all flesh foods (such as meat, poultry, wild game, seafood, and their products). Within the broad category of vegetarian diets, there are several common subtypes (Melina, 2016):

- Vegan diets, which exclude eggs and dairy products
- Lacto-vegetarian diets, which include dairy products but not egg products
- Lacto-ovo-vegetarian diets, which include eggs and dairy products
- Ovo-vegetarian diets, which include egg products but not dairy products

Benefits
- Reduced risk for heart disease, certain cancers, hypertension, diabetes, renal disease, and obesity.

- Improved microbiome, gut health, and increased immunity.
- A diet rich in vegetables, fruits, whole grains, legumes, nuts, and seeds, may increase your intake of fiber, vitamins, minerals, antioxidants.

Considerations

- Nutrient deficiencies: A poorly planned plant-based diet will be deficient in vitamins B12, D, calcium, iron, and omega 3's. Being conscious of your food choices, and if necessary, supplementation can prevent deficiencies.
- Vegans should take 50-100 mcg B12 daily.
- Increased intake of processed foods like chips, pastries, bread, sweetened beverages, cheese, frozen meals, cereals, added sugar, fat, and sodium.
- Digestive issues: The increase in fiber intake, especially if it's sudden, can cause gas, bloating, stomach pain.

How to Get Started

- Eat two meatless meals the first week. Then increase the number of meatless meals weekly. Good options for protein include beans, peas, lentils, nuts, seeds, tofu, or soy.
- Slowly (4-6 weeks) increase the amount of fiber you eat. Drink plenty of fluids. Set a goal of at least 8-10 cups per day. Fluid helps the body process fiber without discomfort.
- Strive for 5 – Eat ½ plate of vegetables with lunch and dinner daily. Especially non-starchy vegetables like broccoli, spinach, kale, Bok Choy, collard greens, Swiss chard just to name a few. Include one serving of fruit with each snack.

- Be adventurous – Try restaurants that specialize in vegetarian cuisine. Purchase a cookbook or browse the internet for new recipes.

References

Melina V, Craig W, Levin S. Position of the Academy of Nutrition and Dietetics: Vegetarian diets. J *Acad Nutr Diet*. 2016; 116(12):1970-1980.

WEEK 12

REFLECTION &
FORWARD PLANNING

WEEK 12

REFLECTION AND FORWARD PLANNING

Closing One Chapter, Opening Another

The journey of professional development doesn't end after 90 days—it's a continuous process of learning, growing, and planning for what's next. Reflection helps you recognize progress, celebrate wins, and identify areas for further improvement. Forward planning ensures that you stay proactive, setting the stage for long-term success.

Consider David, an IT manager who started his 90-day journey feeling overwhelmed and reactive. By the end of the program, he not only developed stronger time management and leadership skills but also set ambitious yet achievable goals for the next phase of his career.

This week, we'll focus on reflecting on your journey and creating a roadmap for sustained growth.

The Importance of Reflection

1. Recognizing Achievements

Reflection allows you to appreciate how far you've come. Celebrating milestones—big or small—boosts motivation and confidence.

- Ask yourself:
  - What goals did I achieve over the past 90 days?
  - How have I grown personally and professionally?

2. Identifying Lessons Learned

Every experience, whether successful or challenging, offers valuable lessons.

- What worked well, and why?
- What obstacles did I encounter, and how did I overcome them?
- What could I do differently next time?

Example: Lisa, a junior architect, realized through reflection that delegating tasks improved her team's efficiency and reduced her own stress.

Practical Reflection Techniques

1. Journaling

Write about your experiences, insights, and feelings.

- Use prompts like:
  - "The most significant lesson I learned is…"
  - "One habit that helped me succeed was…"

2. Feedback Analysis

Review feedback you've received from colleagues, mentors, or clients.

- Look for recurring themes that highlight strengths or areas for growth.

3. Self-Assessment Tools

Use frameworks like SWOT analysis (Strengths, Weaknesses, Opportunities, Threats) to evaluate your position and potential.

The Power of Forward Planning

Reflection is incomplete without action. Forward planning translates insights into strategies for continued success.

1. Setting Long-Term Goals

Define where you want to be in 1, 3, or 5 years.

- Use SMART goals to ensure clarity and focus.
- Example: "Earn a project management certification within the next 12 months to qualify for leadership roles."

2. Breaking Goals into Phases

Large goals can feel daunting unless broken into manageable steps.

- Phase 1: Research certification programs.
- Phase 2: Enroll in a course and allocate weekly study time.
- Phase 3: Complete the certification and update your resume.

3. Creating an Actionable Plan

- Use tools like to-do lists, Gantt charts, or productivity apps to stay organized.
- Schedule regular check-ins with yourself to track progress.

Sustaining Growth Through Reflection and Adaptation

1. Embrace Continuous Learning

Stay curious and proactive about acquiring new skills.

- Identify emerging trends in your industry and explore related opportunities.
- Example: Subscribe to industry newsletters, attend webinars, or join professional groups.

2. Build on Your Network

Nurture the connections you've made during the 90-day journey.

- Schedule periodic catch-ups or send updates about your progress.
- Leverage your network to discover new opportunities or collaborate on projects.

3. Stay Flexible

Life and careers rarely follow a linear path. Be ready to adapt your plans as circumstances change.

- Ask: "What adjustments can I make to align with new opportunities or challenges?"

Storytelling Example: Reflection in Action

Sam, a mid-level analyst, began his 90-day journey struggling with confidence and direction. Through consistent goal-setting, networking, and skill-building, he grew into a more assertive and capable professional.

At the end of the program, Sam used reflection to identify three key takeaways:

1. Confidence in communication led to stronger relationships.
2. Prioritizing time helped him stay productive and balanced.
3. Seeking feedback improved his performance significantly.

Sam then set forward-planning goals to transition into a management role, including mentoring junior colleagues and enrolling in a leadership course. Within a year, he achieved his goal, crediting the habits developed during the 90-day journey.

Conclusion: Looking Back, Moving Forward

The end of this program is only the beginning of a lifelong commitment to growth. By reflecting on your progress and planning for the future, you'll stay focused, adaptable, and ready to tackle new challenges.

This week, challenge yourself to:

1. Reflect on three key achievements or lessons from the past 90 days.

2. Write down one long-term goal and create an actionable plan to achieve it.

Remember, success is a journey, not a destination. Your dedication to reflection and forward planning will ensure that you continue to grow, achieve, and thrive in the years to come.

WEEK 12 CHALLENGE
Reflection and Forward Planning

Visual Guide: Reflection Grid

Category	Reflection
Achievements	List 3 successes from the past 90 days.
Lessons Learned	Write 3 key takeaways from challenges.
Next Steps	Identify one long-term goal and 3 actionable steps.

Checklist:

- Reflect on your top 3 achievements.
- Write a long-term goal with actionable steps.
- Share your reflections with a mentor or colleague.

MINDFUL MOTION:
THE ART OF LIVING WELL

Promoting balanced nutrition and active habits in children.

Affirmation
I enjoy eating foods that make me strong and healthy.

Motivational Quote
"A healthy outside starts from the inside." Robert Urich

Promoting healthy nutrition and active habits in children is crucial for their physical and mental development, as well as for laying the foundation for lifelong health. By focusing on balanced nutrition and encouraging physical activity, families can help their children grow strong, energetic, and healthy. Here are key strategies to foster a healthy lifestyle for kids:

Provide a Balanced Diet - A balanced diet includes a variety of foods from all the food groups to ensure that children get the nutrients they need to grow and thrive. The recommended eating schedule for meals/snacks is every 3-4 hours. Use plates that are 7-9 inches in diameter.

- Vegetables Fruits and Fruit - Aim to fill ¼ - ½ the plate with a colorful variety of vegetables, and ¼ or less of the plate with fruits.
- Whole Grains - Choose ¼ plate of whole grains like brown rice, whole wheat bread, oats, and quinoa over refined grains.

- Lean Proteins - Include ¼ plate of lean protein, such as chicken, fish, beans, tofu, eggs, and nuts.
- Healthy Fats - Incorporate healthy fats from sources like cheese, avocados, and peanut butter the size of your child's whole thumb.
- Dairy or Alternatives - Include 1 cup of low-fat dairy products like milk, yogurt, or fortified plant-based alternatives like almond milk or soy milk.

Establish Regular Mealtimes

- Consistency - Serve meals at regular times each day to help children develop healthy eating habits and avoid overeating or snacking excessively.
- Family Meals - Eating together as a family promotes healthy eating and gives children an opportunity to model good behavior.

Encourage Hydration

- Water is Key - Water should be the primary drink. Encourage kids to drink water regularly throughout the day, as it helps maintain hydration, supports digestion, and keeps their energy levels up. Limit sugary drinks like soda and juice, as they can contribute to weight gain and tooth decay.
- Healthy Drink Alternatives - If kids are looking for something flavored, try infusing water with fruits like lemon, berries, or cucumber to make it more appealing without added sugars.

Involve Kids in Meal Preparation

- Teach Cooking Skills: Involving children in meal planning and preparation helps them learn about healthy foods and fosters a sense of accomplishment. Let them help with washing vegetables, stirring ingredients, or setting the table.
- Gardening: If possible, grow a small vegetable or herb garden together. Children who are involved in growing their own food are often more likely to eat fruits and vegetables.

Encourage Physical Activity

- Make Exercise Fun: Encourage children to engage in physical activities they enjoy. Whether it's dancing, biking, swimming, or playing a sport, finding activities that are fun makes it more likely that children will stay active. Children aged 5-18 should engage in 60 minutes of moderate to vigorous exercise daily.
- Family Activities: Set aside time for family activities like walks, hikes, or sports. This not only keeps everyone moving but also strengthens family bonds and teaches children the importance of staying active.
- Limit Screen Time: Reduce sedentary behaviors, such as watching TV or playing video games, by setting limits on screen time. Encourage outdoor play or creative activities instead.

A healthy diet and regular physical activity contribute to a child's emotional well-being, growth, development, and joy. Encouraging these habits at an early age helps children form positive, lasting behaviors that will benefit them for years to come.

YOUR 90-DAY JOURNEY: A SUMMARY OF GROWTH AND POTENTIAL

Introduction: A Journey of Transformation

Congratulations! Over the past 90 days, you've embarked on a transformative journey of professional development. Through reflection, practice, and dedication, you've cultivated essential skills that position you for lasting success. Whether you aimed to communicate with confidence, lead with purpose, or build a personal brand, each week has provided tools and strategies to help you grow into the best version of yourself.

This summary revisits key lessons from each week, highlights actionable takeaways, and inspires you to continue this journey of lifelong improvement.

Key Takeaways: Building Foundations for Success

1. Communication: The Foundation of Influence

In Week 1, you discovered that confident communication is not about speaking the loudest—it's about clarity, authenticity, and connection. By mastering verbal and non-verbal cues, practicing active listening, and embracing assertiveness, you've unlocked the power to express your ideas effectively.

Inspiration: Think of communication as a bridge between your thoughts and the world. Build that bridge with intention, and you'll inspire trust, collaboration, and action.

2. Productivity: Working Smarter, Not Harder

Week 2 introduced you to time management techniques, like the Eisenhower Matrix, that prioritize impact over busyness. By identifying your most critical tasks and creating focus hours, you learned to maximize efficiency and achieve balance.

Key Insight: Productivity isn't about doing everything—it's about doing what matters.

3. Relationships: Networking with Purpose

In Week 3, you reframed networking as building genuine relationships. Whether through thoughtful outreach, meaningful conversations, or strategic follow-ups, you now understand that connections are the foundation of professional growth.

Actionable Tip: Focus on quality, not quantity. One meaningful relationship can open doors that hundreds of shallow connections cannot.

4. Goal Setting: Charting the Path to Success

Week 4 empowered you to turn aspirations into actionable steps using SMART goals. By aligning goals with your values, breaking them into manageable parts, and tracking progress, you've developed a system to achieve more with purpose.

Inspiration: A goal without a plan is just a wish. You've learned to plan with precision and act with determination.

Key Takeaways: Developing Leadership and Adaptability

5. Active Listening and Empathy: The Heart of Leadership

In Week 5, you discovered that leadership begins with listening and understanding. By practicing active listening and responding with empathy, you've built trust and collaboration in your professional relationships.

Inspiration: Great leaders don't just speak—they listen deeply and act thoughtfully.

6. Feedback: A Tool for Growth

Week 6 helped you view feedback as a gift rather than a critique. Whether giving feedback with the SBI model or receiving it with curiosity, you've learned to make feedback a cornerstone of continuous improvement.

Actionable Tip: Make feedback part of your routine. Seek it regularly, act on it intentionally, and watch your growth accelerate.

7. Managing Up: Supporting Leadership

In Week 7, you explored the art of managing up aligning with your leader's goals, adapting to their style, and proactively offering solutions. By fostering this alignment, you've positioned yourself as a valued partner in the workplace.

Inspiration: Managing up isn't about flattery; it's about collaboration. When leaders thrive, so do their teams.

8. Resilience and Adaptability: Thriving in Change

Week 8 reminded you that challenges are opportunities in disguise. By cultivating resilience and embracing change, you've strengthened your ability to adapt, innovate, and excel in uncertain environments.

Key Insight: Life is 10% what happens to you and 90% how you respond. Choose growth.

Key Takeaways: Personal Branding and Lifelong Growth

9. Personal Branding: Owning Your Narrative

In Week 9, you crafted a personal brand that highlights your strengths, values, and unique contributions. Whether through a polished LinkedIn profile or meaningful posts, you've positioned yourself as a trusted expert in your field.

Inspiration: Your personal brand is the story you tell the world—make it compelling, authentic, and impactful.

10. Lifelong Learning: The Growth Mindset

Week 10 inspired you to adopt a lifelong learning mindset. By identifying skill gaps, leveraging resources, and seeking experiences that stretch you, you've committed to staying curious and competitive in an ever-changing world.

Key Insight: Never stop learning. Growth doesn't have an expiration date.

11. Integrity and Purpose: Leading Authentically

In Week 11, you defined your leadership purpose and aligned your actions with your values. By leading with integrity, you've built trust and set an example for others to follow.

Inspiration: Leadership isn't a title—it's a legacy. Leave one rooted in integrity and purpose.

12. Reflection and Forward Planning: The Cycle of Growth

Week 12 brought everything full circle, encouraging you to reflect on your journey and plan for the future. By celebrating achievements, learning from challenges, and setting new goals, you've ensured that growth becomes a lifelong habit.

Key Insight: Reflection fuels progress. Make it a regular practice to evaluate, adjust, and excel.

Looking Ahead: Inspiration to Excel

As you move forward, remember that your potential is limitless. The tools, strategies, and insights you've gained over these 90 days are just the beginning.

- **Embrace Challenges**
  Every obstacle is an opportunity to grow stronger. Trust in your ability to adapt, overcome, and innovate.

- **Stay Curious**
  The world is full of possibilities for those willing to explore. Keep learning, experimenting, and   pushing boundaries.

- **Lead with Purpose**
  Whether leading a team or guiding your own career, act with intention. Align your actions with   your values, and you'll inspire others to do the same.

A Final Thought: Excellence is a journey

Excellence isn't achieved overnight—it's the result of consistent effort, reflection, and resilience. As you continue your journey, remember the progress you've made and the possibilities that lie ahead.

The great philosopher Aristotle once said, "We are what we repeatedly do. Excellence, then, is not an act, but a habit." Over the past 90 days, you've built habits of excellence. Now, it's time to take them forward and create the future you envision.

Here's to your continued growth, success, and impact. **You've got this!**

Weekly Journal Notes

Journal writing can be a powerful tool for self-reflection and personal growth. To get the most out of your journaling practice, set aside a specific time each day to write, creating a routine that fits your schedule. Start with a clear intention or prompt to guide your thoughts and write honestly without self-editing or judgment. Focus on your experiences, feelings, and insights, exploring both positive and challenging aspects of your day.

_____

_____

_____

_____

_____

_____

_____

_____

_____

_____

_____

BONUS

UNWRITTEN RULES
OF COMPANY
CULTURE

UNWRITTEN RULES OF COMPANY CULTURE

Interpersonal Relationships

1. **Respect Hierarchies While Building Connections:** Understand the formal reporting structures, but don't hesitate to build genuine relationships with colleagues across all levels.
2. **Know When to Speak Up and When to Listen:** Timing and tone are crucial. Sharing ideas is encouraged but understanding the dynamics of when to assert yourself versus when to observe is key.
3. **Don't Overstep Boundaries:** While being approachable is good, avoid prying into personal matters unless a colleague volunteers to share.

Communication Etiquette

4. **Adapt Your Communication Style:** Match your tone and formality to the recipient's preferences, whether it's email, chat, or in-person discussions.
5. **Understand the Power of the "CC":** Use email CCs sparingly to avoid overwhelming others but know when it's necessary to loop in stakeholders.

6. **Prompt Responses Matter:** Timely replies, even if brief, show respect for others' time and needs.
7. **Learn Unspoken Meeting Etiquette:** Be punctual, prepared, and aware of the power dynamics in the room. Some companies expect active participation; others value reserved listening.

Workplace Norms

8. **Understand Work Hours Flexibility:** Observe how strictly people adhere to start and end times. Even in flexible environments, showing consistent availability during core hours is often expected.
9. **Lunch and Break Norms:** Learn whether taking lunch at your desk, in a group, or outside is the norm and how often breaks are typically taken.
10. **"Face Time" Expectations:** Gauge whether staying late is necessary to show commitment, even if your tasks are done.

Performance Expectations

11. **Results vs. Effort:** Some cultures prioritize visible hard work (e.g., staying late), while others care only about deliverables.
12. **Unwritten Dress Code:** Even in casual workplaces, know when to "dress up" for client meetings, presentations, or special events.
13. **Office Politics:** Avoid being openly critical of leadership or colleagues—most workplaces value diplomacy over blunt honesty.

Conflict Resolution

14. **Handle Disputes Discreetly:** Escalating issues openly or too quickly can be frowned upon. Try resolving conflicts directly before involving higher-ups.
15. **Don't Air Grievances Publicly:** Complaining in common spaces, even casually, can negatively impact your reputation.

Professional Growth

16. **Understand Networking Nuances:** Internal networking is often as valuable as external networking. Build allies within your team and beyond.
17. **Know the Path to Promotion:** Beyond performance, observe what behaviors or relationships helped others succeed.
18. **Shadow Decision-Making Processes:** Pay attention to how decisions are made—whether by consensus, individual authority, or behind closed doors.

Social Dynamics

19. **Participate in Company Events Strategically:** Attend team-building activities, but gauge how much socializing is genuinely valued versus obligatory.
20. **Be Careful with Humor:** Workplace humor varies greatly by culture. Stick to neutral topics until you fully understand what's acceptable.

Workplace Tools and Practices

21. **Learn How Tools Are Really Used:** Understand whether systems like project management software are actively followed or just for appearances.
22. **Unwritten Feedback Channels:** Some feedback happens formally; other times, casual comments carry significant weight.

Adapt to Leadership Styles

23. **Follow Your Manager's Lead:** Observe your manager›s preferred working and communication styles. Mimic their priorities for a smoother workflow.
24. **Anticipate Leadership Expectations:** Proactively offer updates or solutions based on past patterns in leadership behavior.

Building Trust and Credibility

25. **Follow Through on Commitments:** Reliability is often judged by small actions like meeting deadlines or delivering quality work.
26. **Don't Overpromise:** Consistency is valued over exaggerated claims of what you can deliver.
27. **Confidentiality Matters:** Respect private discussions and sensitive company information—even casual leaks can damage trust.

Unspoken Loyalty Signals

28. **Avoid Gossip:** Being discreet about sensitive matters builds credibility and trust.
29. **Show Enthusiasm for Key Projects:** Leaders notice when you align your energy with company goals.
30. **Be a Team Player:** Offer help without being asked, especially during crunch times or critical moments.

Understanding and mastering these unwritten rules of company culture often determines how quickly you integrate into a workplace and how effectively you build lasting professional relationships. Success often depends as much on navigating these nuances as on excelling in your job responsibilities.

Final Remarks

As you reflect on your 90-day journey, take a moment to assess your key takeaways and consider how you can leverage these insights for continuous growth. What strategies or habits have proven effective? How can you build upon these learnings to achieve your long-term goals? Reflection is a powerful tool, not only for acknowledging your progress but also for aligning your actions with your aspirations.

Maintaining a balance between work and overall wellness is essential to sustaining success. This includes prioritizing both your physical and mental health, ensuring that your professional achievements do not come at the expense of your personal well-being. Equally important is defining what success looks like for you in your career journey. Take the time to identify clear milestones and actionable steps that will steadily move you closer to your aspirations.

Throughout our professional career, we have observed countless cycles of career missteps and missed opportunities. These often stem from a lack of preparation, such as not knowing the right thing to say or do in unfamiliar or challenging situations. Navigating these complexities requires foresight, strategy, and the ability to adapt to various circumstances.

One of the most effective ways to overcome these challenges is by seeking out mentorship. In today's workforce, having the right mentor is not just beneficial—it's critical. A skilled mentor can help you navigate the intricate dynamics of corporate politics, avoid common pitfalls, and cultivate the skills needed to thrive in a professional community. Furthermore, mentorship fosters an environment where individuals and teams can grow together, creating a culture of collaboration and shared success.

If you're seeking guidance on developing a holistic approach to personal and professional wellness—or if you'd like to explore how mentorship can transform your career—don't hesitate to connect. Together, we can create a strategy to help you thrive both personally and professionally. For more information, feel free to reach out at <u>tracy@lifequalityrd.net</u> and theleadershipwise.com.

BONUS

DETAILED CAREER
PROGRESSION PLAN

DETAILED CAREER PROGRESSION PLAN

A structured career progression plan is essential for advancing in your professional journey. It helps you set clear goals, develop necessary skills, and strategically position yourself for growth opportunities. Below is a detailed, step-by-step plan to guide your career progression:

Step 1: Self-Assessment and Reflection

Goal: Understand your strengths, weaknesses, values, and career aspirations.

1. **Assess Your Current Position**:
   - Identify where you stand in your career. Ask:
     - What are my current responsibilities?
     - What are my achievements in this role?
     - What challenges do I face?
2. **Clarify Your Career Vision**:
   - Define your short-term (1–2 years), mid-term (3–5 years), and long-term (5–10 years) career goals. Be specific:
     - Short-term: "Master project management skills and lead a team project."
     - Mid-term: "Become a department manager and oversee a team of 10."

- Long-term: "Transition to a C-suite position in operations."

3. **Identify Your Core Values**:
   - Reflect on what matters most to you in a career, such as work-life balance, financial success, personal growth, or making an impact.
4. **Use Assessment Tools**:
   - Leverage tools like:
     - Myers-Briggs Type Indicator (MBTI): For personality insights.
     - Clifton Strengths: To identify your unique talents.
     - SWOT Analysis: To identify Strengths, Weaknesses, Opportunities, and Threats.

Step 2: Research Career Opportunities

Goal: Explore potential career paths and opportunities in your field.

1. **Understand Your Industry Landscape**:
   - Research trends, in-demand skills, and growth areas in your industry.
   - Read trade publications, follow industry leaders on social media, and attend webinars or conferences.
2. **Identify Role Models**:
   - Find professionals who have achieved what you aspire to. Study their career trajectories to identify steps you can replicate.
3. **Map Out Potential Career Paths**:
   - For example, if you're in marketing:

- Entry-level: Marketing Coordinator.
- Mid-level: Marketing Manager or Digital Strategist.
- Senior-level: Director of Marketing or Chief Marketing Officer.

4. **Seek Guidance**:
   - Talk to mentors, career coaches, or colleagues to gain insights into career opportunities and advice on navigating transitions.

Step 3: Skill Development

Goal: Acquire the skills and competencies needed to advance.

1. **Identify Skill Gaps**:
   - Compare your current skill set with the requirements for your desired roles.
   - Common skills to focus on:
     - Leadership and management.
     - Technical proficiency in tools or software relevant to your industry.
     - Soft skills like communication, emotional intelligence, and problem-solving.
2. **Pursue Continuous Learning**:
   - Enroll in relevant courses, certifications, or degree programs. Examples:
     - Leadership: Harvard Business School Online or LinkedIn Learning courses.
     - Technical: Certifications like AWS, PMP, or Google Analytics.

- General: Platforms like Coursera, Udemy, and edX.
3. **Leverage On-the-Job Learning**:
   - Volunteer for stretch assignments or cross-functional projects that expose you to new skills and challenges.
4. **Join Professional Organizations**:
   - Participate in industry associations to access resources, training, and networking opportunities.

Step 4: Networking and Relationship Building

Goal: Build a strong professional network to uncover opportunities and gain support.

1. **Strengthen Internal Relationships**:
   - Cultivate strong relationships with colleagues, supervisors, and other departments. These connections can lead to mentorship and internal promotions.
2. **Expand Your External Network**:
   - Attend industry events, join online forums, and participate in networking groups on platforms like LinkedIn or Meetup.
   - Engage with peers by sharing insights, contributing to discussions, and offering help.
3. **Find Mentors and Sponsors**:
   - A mentor provides guidance and advice, while a sponsor actively advocates for your growth. Build relationships with individuals who can fulfill these roles.

4. **Build Your Personal Brand**:
   - Share thought leadership content, showcase your expertise on LinkedIn, and participate in public speaking opportunities to establish credibility.

Step 5: Set Goals and Create a Timeline

Goal: Establish actionable goals and deadlines to guide your progression.

1. **Use SMART Goals**:
   - Specific: Define exactly what you want to achieve.
   - Measurable: Ensure progress can be tracked.
   - Achievable: Set realistic targets based on your capabilities.
   - Relevant: Align goals with your career vision.
   - Time-bound: Set clear deadlines.
2. **Break Down Goals into Milestones**:
   - Example: If your goal is to become a project manager in two years:
     - Month 1: Enroll in a project management course.
     - Month 6: Complete certification.
     - Month 12: Lead a small project team.
3. **Create a Career Progression Plan**:
   - Document your goals, required skills, and steps for achieving each milestone.
   - Regularly review and adjust your plan to reflect new opportunities or changing priorities.

Step 6: Seek Feedback and Evaluate Progress

Goal: Continuously improve by reflecting on achievements and areas for growth.

1. **Solicit Feedback**:
   o Regularly seek feedback from managers, peers, and mentors. Ask:
      - "What are my strengths, and how can I build on them?"
      - "What areas should I focus on improving?"
      - "How can I better contribute to the team?"
2. **Conduct Self-Assessments**:
   o Reflect on your performance at regular intervals. Use questions like:
      - "What have I accomplished this quarter?"
      - "What challenges did I face, and how did I address them?"
3. **Adjust Your Plan**:
   o Based on feedback and self-assessments, refine your career plan to stay on track.

Step 7: Build a Reputation of Excellence

Goal: Establish yourself as a reliable, high-performing professional.

1. **Consistently Deliver Results**:
   o Focus on excelling in your current role by meeting deadlines, exceeding expectations, and maintaining high-quality work.

2. **Take Initiative:**
   o Volunteer for new responsibilities or suggest innovative ideas to solve problems or improve processes.
3. **Develop a Strong Work Ethic:**
   o Demonstrate commitment, reliability, and accountability in everything you do.
4. **Stay Positive and Resilient:**
   o Approach challenges with optimism and a growth mindset, inspiring those around you.

Step 8: Transition to New Roles

Goal: Move into higher-level positions that align with your long-term vision.

1. **Position Yourself for Promotion:**
   o Communicate your interest in growth opportunities to your manager.
   o Share your achievements and readiness for new challenges during performance reviews.
2. **Explore Lateral Moves:**
   o Consider lateral moves to gain diverse experiences and skills, positioning yourself for future promotions.
3. **Apply Strategically:**
   o If pursuing external opportunities, tailor your resume and cover letter to highlight how your experience aligns with the role.
4. **Negotiate Effectively:**
   o When transitioning roles, negotiate compensation and benefits that reflect your value and align with your goals.

Step 9: Plan for Long-Term Success

Goal: Sustain growth and maintain alignment with your evolving goals.

1. **Continue Lifelong Learning**:
   - Stay current with industry trends and continuously update your skills.
2. **Evaluate and Reassess Goals**:
   - Regularly revisit your career vision to ensure it reflects your evolving priorities and aspirations.
3. **Mentor Others**:
   - Share your knowledge and experiences to help others grow, solidifying your reputation as a leader.
4. **Leave a Legacy**:
   - Strive to make a lasting impact in your field, whether by contributing to innovations, fostering a positive culture, or mentoring future leaders.

Career progression is an ongoing journey that requires self-awareness, planning, and adaptability. By following this detailed plan, you can identify your goals, develop essential skills, build meaningful relationships, and position yourself for sustained success. Stay committed to your growth, embrace challenges as opportunities, and take deliberate steps toward achieving the career of your dreams.

ABOUT THE AUTHORS

Dr. Tenia Davis is an accomplished Human Resources practitioner and an award winning author with extensive executive leadership experience in highcaliber organizations, currently serving as the Chief People Officer, NORC at the University of Chicago . She holds an MS, MBA and a PhD in Values-Driven Leadership, specializing in talent acquisition, operational excellence, change management, and diversity initiatives. Known for her global business acumen and commitment to developing future leaders, Tenia has earned recognition for her transformative impact in the field.

With over 30 years of experience in the health and fitness industry as a Registered Dietitian and Personal Trainer, Tracy Granberry, RDN has dedicated her career to empowering individuals to fuel their bodies and souls through proper nutrition and regular exercise. Tracy's passion lies in creating personalized diet and fitness programs tailored to each person's unique needs and goals.

Whether you're striving to manage a chronic condition, lose weight, boost athletic performance, or simply feel your best, Tracy's approach combines expertise and a deep commitment to help you achieve maximum results efficiently and effectively. Tracy's focus plan will unlock your potential and craft a healthier, more vibrant you.

Weekly Journal Notes

Journal writing can be a powerful tool for self-reflection and personal growth. To get the most out of your journaling practice, set aside a specific time each day to write, creating a routine that fits your schedule. Start with a clear intention or prompt to guide your thoughts and write honestly without self-editing or judgment. Focus on your experiences, feelings, and insights, exploring both positive and challenging aspects of your day.

_____

_____

_____

_____

_____

_____

_____

_____

_____

_____

Weekly Journal Notes

Journal writing can be a powerful tool for self-reflection and personal growth. To get the most out of your journaling practice, set aside a specific time each day to write, creating a routine that fits your schedule. Start with a clear intention or prompt to guide your thoughts and write honestly without self-editing or judgment. Focus on your experiences, feelings, and insights, exploring both positive and challenging aspects of your day.

_____

_____

_____

_____

_____

_____

_____

_____

_____

_____

_____

_____

Weekly Journal Notes

Journal writing can be a powerful tool for self-reflection and personal growth. To get the most out of your journaling practice, set aside a specific time each day to write, creating a routine that fits your schedule. Start with a clear intention or prompt to guide your thoughts and write honestly without self-editing or judgment. Focus on your experiences, feelings, and insights, exploring both positive and challenging aspects of your day.

Weekly Journal Notes

Journal writing can be a powerful tool for self-reflection and personal growth. To get the most out of your journaling practice, set aside a specific time each day to write, creating a routine that fits your schedule. Start with a clear intention or prompt to guide your thoughts and write honestly without self-editing or judgment. Focus on your experiences, feelings, and insights, exploring both positive and challenging aspects of your day.

Weekly Journal Notes

Journal writing can be a powerful tool for self-reflection and personal growth. To get the most out of your journaling practice, set aside a specific time each day to write, creating a routine that fits your schedule. Start with a clear intention or prompt to guide your thoughts and write honestly without self-editing or judgment. Focus on your experiences, feelings, and insights, exploring both positive and challenging aspects of your day.

_____

_____

_____

_____

_____

_____

_____

_____

_____

_____

_____

_____

Weekly Journal Notes

Journal writing can be a powerful tool for self-reflection and personal growth. To get the most out of your journaling practice, set aside a specific time each day to write, creating a routine that fits your schedule. Start with a clear intention or prompt to guide your thoughts and write honestly without self-editing or judgment. Focus on your experiences, feelings, and insights, exploring both positive and challenging aspects of your day.

_____

_____

_____

_____

_____

_____

_____

_____

_____

_____

_____

_____

Weekly Journal Notes

Journal writing can be a powerful tool for self-reflection and personal growth. To get the most out of your journaling practice, set aside a specific time each day to write, creating a routine that fits your schedule. Start with a clear intention or prompt to guide your thoughts and write honestly without self-editing or judgment. Focus on your experiences, feelings, and insights, exploring both positive and challenging aspects of your day.

_____

_____

_____

_____

_____

_____

_____

_____

_____

_____

_____

_____

Made in the USA
Las Vegas, NV
12 January 2025

16174233R00154